Linking Conservation and Poverty Reduction

Linking Conservation and Poverty Reduction

Landscapes, People and Power

Robert Fisher, Stewart Maginnis,
William Jackson, Edmund Barrow and Sally Jeanrenaud
with
Andrew Ingles, Richard Friend, Rati Mehrotra,
Taghi Farvar, Michelle Laurie and Gonzalo Oviedo

publishing for a sustainable future

London • Sterling, VA

First published by Earthscan in the UK and USA in 2008

HB ISBN: 978-1-84407-635-2
PB ISBN: 978-1-84407-636-9
Typeset by Safehouse Creative
Printed and bound in the UK by TJ International Ltd, Padstow
Cover design by Dan Bramall

For a full list of publications please contact:

Earthscan
Dunstan House
14a St Cross St
London, EC1N 8XA, UK
Tel: +44 (0)20 7841 1930
Fax: +44 (0)20 7242 1474
Email: earthinfo@earthscan.co.uk
Web: **www.earthscan.co.uk**

22883 Quicksilver Drive, Sterling, VA 20166-2012, USA

Earthscan publishes in association with the International Institute for Environment and Development

A catalogue record for this book is available from the British Library

Library of Congress Cataloging-in-Publication Data
Linking conservation and poverty reduction : landscapes, people and power / edited by Robert Fisher ... [et al.].
     p. cm
  "The first edition of this book, Poverty and Conservation: Landscapes, People and Power [was] published by IUCN in 2005"–Acknowledgements.
   ISBN 978-1-84407-635-2 (hbk.)–ISBN 978-1-84407-639-9 (pbk.) 1. Rural poor. 2. Rural development–Citizen participation. 3. Sustainable development. I. Fisher, R. J. II. Povery and conservation.
   HC79.P6P6826 2008
   338.9'07–dc22

                                                                     2008028394

FSC
Mixed Sources
Product group from well-managed
forests and other controlled sources
Cert no. SGS-COC-2482
www.fsc.org
© 1996 Forest Stewardship Council

Contents

List of Figures, Tables and Boxes

Figures

Tables

Boxes

About the Authors

Edmund Barrow is coordinator of Forest Conservation and the Livelihoods and Landscapes Strategy for IUCN in Africa.

Taghi Farvar of the Centre for Sustainable Development, Iran (CENESTA) is the chair of IUCN's Commission on Environmental, Economic and Social Policy (CEESP) and the executive secretary of the World Alliance of Mobile Indigenous Peoples (WAMIP).

Robert Fisher, senior researcher at the Australian Mekong Resource Centre at the University of Sydney, is an anthropologist specializing in natural resource management and particularly in community forestry.

Richard Friend previously worked for IUCN in the Lao PDR, and is now scientist – Fisheries Institutions & Policy for the Greater Mekong Region at the WorldFish Center.

Andrew Ingles is coordinator of Forest Conservation and the Livelihoods and Landscapes Strategy for IUCN in Asia.

William Jackson is deputy director general of IUCN and co-author of *Forest Quality* (2006, Earthscan).

Sally Jeanrenaud is coordinator of the Future of Sustainability Initiative at IUCN.

Michelle Laurie worked with the IUCN Forest Conservation Programme from 2003 to 2007, and now works with local and international organizations to improve their capacity to collaborate, learn and share knowledge more effectively.

Stewart Maginnis has worked in sustainable forest management and community forestry for over 20 years in Africa, Latin America and Europe, and now heads the International Union for Conservation of Nature (IUCN) Forest Conservation

Programme in Switzerland. He is co-editor of *Forests in Landscapes* (2005, Earthscan) and *The Forest Landscape Restoration Handbook* (2007, Earthscan).

Rati Mehrotra, formerly environmental economics and social equity officer at IUCN, is the managing partner of M-Power Services and NSOE fellow at Duke University, US.

Gonzalo Oviedo, an anthropologist and environmentalist from Ecuador, is senior adviser on social policy at IUCN, where he leads the Conservation for Poverty Reduction Initiative.

Case study authors

Deborah Barry is a senior research associate with the Center for International Forestry Research working on forest policy, tenure and rights and participatory development.

Peter Cronkleton is an anthropologist working for the Center for International Forestry Research specializing in community forestry, participatory development and forest policy.

Stephanie Duvail is a geographer, working for the French Institute of Research for Development (IRD) and specializing in floods and livelihoods in tropical floodplains.

Olivier Hamerlynck is a medical doctor and ecologist and works as an independent consultant associated with the Centre for Ecology and Hydrology (Wallingford) on ecosystem management.

Jaruwan Kaewmahanin previously worked with the Thailand Outreach Program of the Regional Community Forestry Training Center for Asia and the Pacific (RECOFTC) in Thailand and now works with the Mangrove Action Project (MAP) Asia office in Trang, Thailand.

Sounthone Ketpanh is a senior officer in the Department of Forestry in the Lao PDR and was project manager of the National Agriculture and Forestry Research Institute (NAFRI), International Union for Conservation of Nature (IUCN), Non-timber Forest Products (NTFP) Project.

Peter Leigh Taylor is an associate professor in the Sociology Department at Colorado State University.

Wendolin Mlenge, a forester, has worked as the project manager of Hifadhi Ardhi Shiyanga – Soil Conservation Shinyanga (HASHI) of the Tanzania Forests and Bee Keeping Division, since its inception in 1985.

Jason Morris worked for several years in Southeast Asia and is now studying for his PhD at the University of California, Berkeley.

Somsak Sukwong is a leading supporter of community forestry in Thailand and was the founding director of the Regional Community Forestry Training Centre for Asia and the Pacific.

Acknowledgements

The first edition of this book, *Poverty and Conservation: Landscapes, People and Power*, published by IUCN in 2005, was an outcome of a project on poverty conservation undertaken by the IUCN Forest Conservation Programme in collaboration with the IUCN Eastern Africa Regional Office, the Asian Regional Office and CEESP. The project was supported by IUCN's 3I-C fund, an internal programme development fund set up to promote innovation, integration, information and communication.

We are grateful to the many people who contributed to the rich discussion that surrounded the development of the book, both in the first edition and this second edition. These people came from within IUCN, but also from many other agencies with similar concerns. They included reviewers, participants who attended workshops in Khao Yai, Thailand and the Abedares, Kenya and others: Lorena Aguilar, Ruth Barreto, Joshua Bishop, Guido Broekhoven, Florence Chege, Nigel Dudley, Piyathip Eawpanich, Joanna Elliott, Phil Franks, Samuel Gichere, Don Gilmour, Peter Hazelwood, Frits Hesselink, David Kaimowitz, Margaret Kakande, Ly Oumou Koulsoum, Yam Malla, Mira Lee Manickham, Susan Matindi, Carmel Mbizvo, Jess McLean, Jeff McNeely, Tom McShane, Simon Milledge, Alex Muhweezi, Teresa Mulliken, Paul Noupa, Jean-Yves Pirot, Corli Pretorius, Carole Saint-Laurent, Melita Samoilys, Jeff Sayer, Sandeep Sengupta, Gill Shepherd, Paul Steele, William Sunderlin, Eldad Tukahirwa and Asif Ali Zaindi.

We are grateful to the Directorate General for Development Cooperation of Italy for the support they provided for the preparation of this book.

We would like to express thanks to all of these people and many others who have helped in developing the thinking behind the book.

Foreword

Conservation agencies such as IUCN support conservation of biodiversity both for its intrinsic value and for its importance in providing life support for humans through ecosystem services on which human livelihoods ultimately depend. This dependence on biodiversity applies to all humans including the growing numbers of urban dwellers although it is more directly relevant to the many millions of rural poor who depend directly on natural resources in their daily lives.

It is significant that many of the poorest people in the world live in areas with some of the richest biodiversity. It is also true that areas rich in biodiversity are often rich in cultural diversity. While conservationists need to remain aware of the wider global needs for conservation, focus on the areas of high biodiversity value is a continuing priority. Working in such areas makes it essential that the linkages between poverty and conservation are understood.

There are continuing debates about these linkages and about the role, or potential role, of conservation in contributing to poverty reduction. Some suggest that addressing poverty is a necessary tool for conservation, at least in some circumstances, while others argue that conservation, properly managed, can contribute to poverty reduction. Neither of these positions is totally accepted by all.

This book, originally published by IUCN as *Poverty and Conservation: Landscapes, People and Power*, makes an important conceptual contribution to the understanding of the linkages between poverty and conservation, and more specifically between conservation and poverty *reduction*. One important contribution is the emphasis that simple generalizations about linkages are rarely accurate. For example statements such as 'poverty causes environmental degradation', or 'poverty reduction is essential to conservation' are true only in certain contexts, and causal relationships can be changed by institutional changes and other interventions.

IUCN is deeply committed to poverty reduction both because it can often contribute to effective conservation, but also because we see addressing the issue of global poverty as an ethical imperative to which conservation and sustainable development can, and must, contribute.

This book aims to contribute to the work of conservationists and development specialists who are working towards dual goals of poverty reduction and conservation.

Julia Marton-Lefèvre
Director-General
International Union for Conservation of Nature (IUCN)

List of Acronyms and Abbreviations

ACOFOP	Association of Forest Communities of Petén
APEC	Asia-Pacific Economic Community
CAMPFIRE	Communal Areas Management Programme for Indigenous Resources
CBD	Convention on Biological Diversity
CBNRM	community-based natural resource management
CEESP	Commission on Environmental, Economic and Social Policy
CENESTA	Centre for Sustainable Development, Iran
CICIAFOC	*Asociación Co-ordinadora Indígena y Campesina de Agroforesteria Comunitária de Centroamerica*
CMA	collaborative management area
CMAP	collaborative management area plan
CONAP	National Commission on Protected Areas
DAFO	District Agriculture and Forestry Office
DFID	Department for International Development
DNP	Diawling National Park
FAO	Food and Agriculture Organization
FECOFUN	Federation of Community Forest Users of Nepal
GAD	gender and development
HASHI	*Hifadhi Ardhi Shinyanga* – Soil Conservation Shinyanga
ICCO	Interchurch Organisation for Development Co-operation
ICDP	integrated conservation and development project
IRD	Institute of Research for Development
IUCN	International Union for Conservation of Nature
JFM	joint forest management
KFW	*Kreditanstalt für Wiederaufbau*
LARReC	Living Aquatic Resources Research Centre
MAP	Mangrove Action Project
MBR	Maya Biosphere Reserve
MDG	Millennium Development Goal
MUZ	Multiple Use Zone
NAFRI	National Agriculture and Forestry Research Institute

NTFP   non-timber forest product
OMVS   *Organisation pour la mise en valeur du fleuve Sénégal*
PES   payment for environmental services
PROFOR   Program on Forests (World Bank)
PRSP   poverty reduction strategy paper
RECOFTC   Regional Community Forestry Training Center for Asia and the
            Pacific
TCZCDP   Tanga Coastal Zone Conservation and Development Programme
UNCED   United Nations Conference on Environment and Development
UNDP   United Nations Development Programme
USAID   United States Agency for International Development
WAMIP   World Alliance of Mobile Indigenous Peoples
WCD   World Commission on Dams
WSSD   World Summit on Sustainable Development

1

Introduction

The challenge of sustainable development

In 1992 the United Nations Conference on Environment and Development (UNCED) in Rio de Janeiro captured the world's attention with promises to achieve sustainable development[1] through combined efforts in economics, social development and the environment (commonly referred to as the three 'pillars' of sustainable development). Ten years later, during the World Summit on Sustainable Development (WSSD) in Johannesburg, the international community reaffirmed that sustainable development was an international priority. It stressed the eradication of extreme poverty as the primary goal, as indicated in the Millennium Development Goals (MDGs) (see Box 1.1).[2] The 2005 World Summit again reaffirmed international support for the MDGs (General Assembly of the United Nations, 2005).

The WSSD also highlighted the fact that success in achieving sustainable development has been mixed at best. World Bank figures show scant progress on some poverty indicators. Although there is some improvement in the percentage of people living on less than US$1 per day (29.6 per cent in 1990; 23.2 per cent in 1999), there are wide regional disparities.[3] Other indicators, such as the HIV/AIDS pandemic, are alarming.[4] The MDGs Report 2006 (United Nations, 2006) reports further improvements, with continuing regional disparities and 'staggering' challenges. In terms of goal seven, ensuring environmental stability, although nearly 12 per cent of the Earth's land area is now designated as Protected Areas (IUCN, 2003), net forest loss continues at ten million hectares per year, wetlands continue to decline, the number of countries with water shortages continues to increase and fisheries continue to be depleted. The picture is not all negative, however. There have been improvements in some areas, such as global food security, but these improvements do not amount to sustainable development.

Thus, in spite of more than ten years of concern with sustainable development, achievements have been relatively limited, attempts to link environmental, economic and social issues in practice have been unimpressive and tangible outcomes of sustainable development programmes and projects have been scarce. Why is this so? Why, in spite of high-level political commitment and considerable expenditure of money and effort, has sustainable development proved so elusive?

Box 1.1 The Millennium Development Goals

1   Eradicate extreme poverty and hunger
2   Achieve universal primary education
3   Promote gender equality and empower women
4   Reduce child mortality
5   Improve maternal health
6   Combat HIV/AIDS, malaria and other diseases
7   Ensure environmental stability
8   Develop a global partnership for development.

Source: UNDP website: www.undp.org/mdg/

The relative lack of progress towards sustainable development is not the result of any fundamental problem with the concept. It is due more to the fact that the real emphasis has been on developing the economy first and hoping that positive social and environmental changes would follow. Although the three pillars of sustainable development (economy, environment and society) were not seen at UNCED as separable, in practice the emphasis has been on the economic pillar. Part of the reason for this has been the increasing dominance of the political agenda by free-market and economic growth models of development in recent years.

While development cannot be achieved without economic growth, the overemphasis on economic development has in many instances undermined the environment in ways that affect the long-term benefits of development. In addition, development activities (such as large dams and mining activities) have often made people worse off, whatever the benefits at larger scales. At the same time, conservation activities have sometimes undermined poverty reduction efforts and even worsened poverty.

Along similar lines to the 'economic development first' approach, it has sometimes been argued that the eradication of poverty should come first and that the environment can be addressed later, but the long-term consequences of such an approach are likely to be very serious (Cole and Neumayer, 2005). An alternative view is that, even if the eradication of poverty and hunger is regarded as the high-priority goal, this cannot be achieved in isolation from achieving environmental stability and meeting social development goals. In this book we argue that the eradication of extreme poverty, and, more broadly, achieving sustainable development are only possible if the interdependency of social development, economics and the environment is recognized and accounted for. More equitable approaches to conservation and development require that attention be paid to the poor, particularly the impacts of poverty reduction strategies, economic development and biodiversity conservation.

This point has been recognized, at least in some quarters, for some time, and since the first edition of this book was published in 2005 there has been increasing concern with the importance of environmental services, the value of biodiversity as a resource for sustainable livelihoods and particularly for poverty reduction, and concern that sustainable poverty reduction depends on careful use of resources. This concern has led to a large number of publications such as WRI (2005), Mainka et al (2005) and People–Environment Partnership (2005, known as the Pearce Report). Kofi Annan, when Secretary General of the United Nations, called for investment in 'better resource management' including ecosystem preservation in a report to the United Nations General Assembly on the 2005 World Summit (United Nations General Assembly, 2005). He pointed out that:

> *Our efforts to defeat poverty and pursue sustainable development will be in vain if environmental degradation and natural resource depletion continue unabated. (p19)*

There have been a number of major initiatives that attempt to address poverty through conservation, including the People–Environment Partnership, the Rights and Resources Initiative (both coalitions of development and conservation agencies) and IUCN's 'Conservation for Poverty Reduction'.[5]

The Millennium Ecosystem Assessment was a major international initiative that commenced in 2001 and involved over 1000 experts. The assessment led to four main findings, all of which establish fundamental connections between healthy ecosystems and human wellbeing. The outcomes were presented in a wide variety of publications. Two of the findings are particularly relevant to a discussion of conservation and poverty (Millennium Ecosystem Assessment, 2005, p1):

> • *The changes that have been made to ecosystems have contributed to substantial net gains in human well-being and economic development, but these gains have been achieved at growing costs in the form of degradation of many ecosystem services, increased risks of nonlinear changes, and the exacerbation of poverty for some groups of people. These problems, unless addressed, will substantially diminish the benefits that future generations obtain from ecosystems.*

- *The degradation of ecosystem services could grow significantly worse during the first half of this century and is a barrier to achieving the Millennium Development Goals.*

In this book, we wish to reinvigorate sustainable development rather than suggest an entirely new approach. We believe this can be done by improving the linkages and balancing the impact of actions in each pillar of sustainable development, particularly on the poor.

The call to reinvigorate sustainable development presents major challenges to the development and conservation communities alike. The challenge to the development community is that, despite many years and large investments, rural poverty remains a major problem: 75 per cent of the poor are rural dwellers (IFAD, 2002). Many development activities have made many people worse off. Whatever the benefits at larger scales, development has often occurred at a cost to the poorest people and the environment. Indeed, the environment has been ignored as an opportunity for poverty reduction and the focus on short-term development at the cost of environmental damage has often undermined longer-term efforts at poverty reduction.

For conservationists, despite many years of effort and some important successes, a biodiversity crisis still exists. Conservationists have largely failed to convince economists and developmental practitioners of conservation's long-term importance to development. Further, in the process of promoting conservation, conservationists have, to a considerable extent, ignored its costs to poor peoples' livelihoods and the inequitable distribution of these costs. Conservationists face three challenges:

1   making a better case for the long-term economic and social benefits of conservation;
2   accounting for the real costs of some conservation activities to the poor;
3   recognizing biodiversity as a livelihood resource as well as a global public good.

While this book calls for the reinvigoration of sustainable development, it focuses particularly on a subset of sustainable development issues: the links between poverty reduction, economic development and biodiversity conservation. The connections between poverty, the economy and the environment are complex and the extent to which conservation activities can and should address poverty issues is still being argued. This, however, does not negate the need for conservationists to do a better job at figuring out how to address poverty, for both ethical and practical reasons.[6]

This book highlights the importance of improving institutional arrangements in ways that build opportunities to reduce poverty and improve conservation. In particular it looks at the importance of creating institutional mechanisms for equitable negotiation about competing objectives for resource use and competing interests. It also argues that thinking of conservation and natural resource management on a landscape scale provides better opportunities to achieve diverse objectives than striving to meet multiple objectives in specific sites. This has particular relevance to protected areas. While protected areas are important to conservation, a more comprehensive package of tools and strategies must be applied, both inside and outside protected areas.

Livelihoods, poverty and conservation

Livelihoods can be thought of as the ways in which people make a living. This is not just a matter for the poor, although sometimes livelihoods are equated with subsistence. Livelihoods contribute to human wellbeing, which includes spiritual and aesthetic values. Poverty can be thought of as a state of reduced or limited livelihood opportunities. This obviously includes tangibles like assets and goods for consumption, but also involves vulnerability and powerlessness to make meaningful choices about livelihoods. Although poverty is often defined in absolute terms (people falling below a specified level of income, commonly US$2 per day), it can also be seen as having multiple dimensions. The World Bank (2001) refers to three dimensions of poverty: lack of assets, powerlessness and vulnerability. This book adopts the World Bank definition. (The concept of poverty is discussed more fully in Chapter 2.)

This book uses the term 'conservation' in its broadest sense, including management of natural resources sustainably as well as their protection and restoration, rather than in the narrow sense of maintaining an original state, or preservation. This is an important distinction. The term is often used by different people to mean quite different things, which creates considerable confusion.

Conserving natural resources can have important direct positive benefits on livelihoods, particularly those of rural people. Natural resources are used for direct consumption and for income generation. (See the cases of Shinyanga and of Pred Nai in Chapter 3.) The economic value of wild resources is often ignored in quantifying rural economy and livelihoods, but it can have considerable importance (see Box 1.2).

Conservation is essential for livelihoods in a variety of ways. In developing countries, maintenance of diverse natural resources can be particularly important in providing livelihood security in times of seasonal shortage (by providing alternative foods and other resources) and in times of crisis, such as drought, crop failure or even market failure (see Box 1.3). Maintaining diverse livelihood options is essential for many of the rural poor. Conservation of natural resources is important in providing secure environmental services (such as water and clean air) to all humans, rural and urban, wealthy or poor. It also provides important insurance against risks, including crop failure, market failure and natural disasters.

Box 1.2 The value of wild resources

The economic value of wild resources in Senegal

An analysis of the value of wild foods and other wild resources in Senegal focused on non-timber forest products, game and freshwater fisheries. It found that, in the surveyed areas, these products were mostly used to generate income. Small amounts were used for home consumption.

Although the value of these products is not included in national accounts, the study concluded that the annual value is between US$19 million and US$35 million. This does not include the value of plant resources such as 'fuelwood, charcoal and building materials, which are equally significant but largely accounted for in national economic statistics'. The study also noted that 'natural resources appear to be more important as a share of total cash income for poorer households'.

The study also presented some important findings on the impacts of gender and education:

> ... female-headed households report less cash income from hunting but more from other wild products and artisanal mining, although the latter differences are not statistically significant. Women also report less cash income in total. Finally, household heads with little or no formal education reported more cash income from gathering wild resources (not hunting) on average, than those who had attended primary school or received [Quranic] instruction.
>
> Source: UDRSS/VALEURS (2002)

The economic value of wildlife

The Department for International Development's study of wildlife and poverty linkages found that poor people are significantly dependent 'on wildlife for livelihood and food security, particularly through bushmeat and tourism'. According to the study '[o]f the estimated 1.2 billion people who live on less than the equivalent of a dollar a day ... as many as 150 million people (one-eighth of the world's poorest) perceive wildlife to be an important livelihood asset'.

Source: DFID (2002)

While it is clear that species gathered from the wild can be important to poor people, especially in times of crisis, some economists point out that poorer households generally have no other livelihood options open to them, and that many would not choose to depend on wild resources for their survival if given a choice. It is precisely because they are so poor that they depend on such safety nets. Instead it is claimed that tying livelihoods and poverty reduction objectives to natural resource conservation creates a 'poverty-trap'. Wunder (2001), for example, argues that the potential of tropical forests to lift people out of poverty is very limited.[7] Dove (1993) argues that forest conservation is unlikely to lead

Box 1.3 Food security and diversity in Laotian forests

In Salavan province, in Lao PDR, the rural diet is dominated by glutinous rice, which contributes 73 per cent of total dietary intake during the rainy seasons. Forest foods are essential components of the diet, accounting for an average of 19 per cent of total dietary intake in the rainy season. Excluding rice, forest foods amount to 70 per cent of dietary intake. As forest foods provide year-round diversity to otherwise bland and poorly balanced diets, they also ensure a regular source of nutrients. Approximately 44 per cent of the total calcium and vitamin A and C intake, 25 per cent of total iron intake and 27 per cent of daily protein requirements come from the forest.

Source: Dechaineux (2001)

to poverty reduction because the poor tend only to have the rights to low-value forest products. Whenever products become valuable, the poor lose access.

We agree that such safety nets must never become poverty traps. However, especially in the absence of functioning social security systems and reliable market networks in rural areas, we maintain that the sustainable use of biological resources will remain crucial to the secure livelihoods of the poor in the foreseeable future. Further, we would stress poverty reduction involves empowerment in the form of altered access to valuable natural resources in order to allow benefits to flow to the poor. Poverty traps are not so much a result of dependence on natural resources as they are a result of lack of access to valuable natural resources.

It is important to note the emerging recognition of the complex connections between poverty and vulnerability to natural disasters: these present another angle on the importance of conservation for poverty reduction. It is increasingly clear that the poor tend to be particularly vulnerable to natural disasters (as the 2004 Asian tsunami made clear) and it is likely that they will be particularly vulnerable to the effects of climate change. Such vulnerability arises from a number of factors:

- The poor are often located in the areas vulnerable to natural disasters;
- the poor are usually not well endowed with economic assets (or insurance) and, in the case of disasters, often lose everything;
- as they depend heavily on natural resources, drastic changes to the environment also drastically affect their livelihood systems;
- reconstruction efforts after natural disasters can also be a problem as the poor lose rights to land and resources, sometimes because they lack formal rights in the first place and sometimes because more powerful people take advantage of a situation, as happened in southern Thailand after the Asian tsunami when a 'private investor used police and soldiers to ... prevent people from accessing their devastated community'. (Kaewkuntee, 2006)

The value of conservation to integrated risk management for natural disasters, and the associated need to consider the particular vulnerability of the poor are increasingly recognized (see for example Sudmeier-Rieux et al, 2006).

Threats to livelihoods from development

Clearly (as illustrated in Box 1.4) natural resources can be very important to livelihood security of rural people. Ineffective economic development policies and practices pursued by governments, sectoral development and large-scale infrastructure projects, and macro-economic reform have all too often jeopardized poor peoples' livelihoods by destroying the resource base.

One example from the Northern Province of Cameroon shows how sectoral development planning can dramatically affect livelihoods and undermine the functions – and the economic value – of natural ecosystems (Box 1.4).

Box 1.4 Effects of irrigation in Cameroon

The Waza Logone floodplain (8000 square kilometres) is a critical area of biodiversity and high productivity in a dry area, where rainfall is uncertain and livelihoods are extremely insecure. The floodplain's natural goods and services provide income and subsistence for more than 85 per cent of the region's rural population, or 125,000 people. The biodiversity and high productivity of the floodplain depend to a large extent on the annual inundation of the Logone River. In 1979 the construction of a small irrigated rice scheme (40 square kilometres) reduced flooding by almost 1000 square kilometres. The socio-economic effects of this loss have been devastating, incurring livelihood costs of almost US$50 million over approximately 20 years. Up to 8000 households have suffered direct economic losses of more than US$2 million a year through reduction in dry-season grazing, fishing, natural resource harvesting and surface water supplies. The losses incurred are far in excess of the anticipated return from irrigation.

After 1994, pilot flood releases were made in the Waza Logone floodplain, unblocking watercourses that had been sealed off as a result of the irrigation scheme. Without altering the operations of the rice scheme, these led to demonstrable recoveries in floodplain flora and fauna over 1000 square kilometres, and have been welcomed by local people. The economic value of the floodplain restoration is immense. Improved planning at the regional scale will rehabilitate vital pasture, fisheries and farmland areas used by nearly a third of the population, with a value of almost US$250 per capita.

Source: Loth (2004)[8]

Large-scale infrastructure development often has negative impacts on the livelihoods of the poor, even though it may provide benefits at a wider scale or for a nation as a whole. The construction of large dams is one example of short-term regional or national economic benefits taking precedence over the rights and long-term livelihood security of the rural poor. As the World Commission on Dams (WCD, 2000, p7) concluded, large dams have often made an 'important and significant contribution to human development', but the costs of securing benefits have been very high and unevenly distributed, with poor and vulnerable groups 'likely to bear a disproportionate share of the social and environmental costs of large dam projects without gaining a commensurate share of the economic benefits' (p17). The WCD argues that a 'balance-sheet' approach to assessing costs and benefits (that is, adding up costs and benefits without looking at the way in which they are distributed) 'is increasingly seen as unacceptable on equity grounds and as a poor means of assessing the "best projects"' (p17).

Threats to livelihoods from conservation

While it is clear that development activities may have unintended negative impacts on the poor or may fail to include the poor as beneficiaries, conservation has sometimes had similar outcomes. Conservation practices can have serious negative effects on livelihoods by limiting access to the resources necessary for subsistence, livelihood security or income generation. One major way in which conservation has been detrimental to the poor is by excluding people from protected areas or limiting their access to resources within protected areas. Such exclusionary practices have serious and well-documented negative outcomes (Brockington, 2003; McLean and Straede, 2003; Brockington and Igoe, 2006), especially when resident people are resettled to other locations. There are very few documented cases where forced resettlement[9] provides adequate alternative livelihoods, and resettled people frequently place additional pressure on those already living in resettlement areas. This applies to forced resettlement resulting from both large-scale development projects (such as dams) and the creation of protected areas. In recent years many conservation projects and programmes have attempted to address some of the negative effects of exclusory practices on people with integrated conservation and development programmes. These initiatives essentially aim to provide alternatives to livelihood-related resources from protected areas. Chapter 2 shows that these projects have had limited success, but they are an important step forward.

It is not conservation itself that is the problem for poor rural people whose livelihoods depend on natural resources. Rather, conservation approaches often do not adequately take into account the adverse impacts of conservation activities on the rural poor. Conservation has often been narrowly interpreted as requiring exclusion of people from resource use. Protected areas provide an important alternative to destructive land uses such as large-scale forest plantations, mining projects and commercial agriculture, which not only have negative environmental impacts but can undermine poor people's livelihood security. Protected areas are not the only, and certainly not the worst, large-scale land use that affects the livelihoods of the rural poor. Nevertheless, it is not good enough to justify processes of exclusion and expropriation of resources on the grounds that others do it.[10] We recognize the need for 'trade-offs'. The point is that interventions often do not even recognize that the costs of these trade-offs are borne by the rural poor, leave alone dealing with the issue in an equitable way.

Causal linkages and their implications

This chapter does not provide a comprehensive review of the linkages between conservation, environmental degradation, poverty and wealth. Clearly these linkages are very complex, although people have a strong tendency to try and demonstrate one-way causal links between various factors. For example, the following often contradictory assertions are all made frequently and often backed up with good evidence (at least for a particular case):

- Poverty leads to increased environmental degradation, either because rural people don't know better or because they have no choice but to overexploit natural resources.
- Wealthy people have a severe impact on natural resources because they consume more. This often leads to environmental degradation.
- People who are dependent on resources for their livelihoods are likely to protect them more carefully.
- Conservation worsens poverty by excluding people from resources.
- Conservation contributes to better quality of livelihoods because it guarantees availability of resources.

All these assertions can be valid interpretations of specific cases, but none of them is true universally.[11] Attempts to understand causal linkages must be related to the contexts of specific situations. The specific factors that govern causes and effects need to be carefully identified and properly understood, a process that will often be quite complex. For example in the case of Shinyanga (Case Study 2, Chapter 3), a change in rights of access to forest resources changed the way people who used forests, despite increasing population. There was no simple relationship between population increase and resource degradation. Further, in the absence of widely applicable causal patterns, addressing poverty and conservation linkages will inevitably be more of an art – requiring creativity and flexibility – than an exact science.

To some extent this view runs contrary to calls for an 'evidence-based approach' to conservation. Sutherland et al (2004) argue that conservation practice is often 'based upon anecdote and myth rather than upon the systemic appraisal of the evidence'. They argue that conservation practitioners can learn from the results of applying the 'evidence-based approach' in medical practice. They make particular reference to work that attempts to link development with conservation:

A major thrust of recent conservation work has been to incorporate socio-economic development, but many of the practices seem based upon faith and a political agenda rather than on the benefits to biodiversity. As examples, does clarifying who owns the property rights to each area result in long-term sustainable development or overexploitation? Does providing alternative sources of income... reduce the need to exploit natural resources, act as an additional activity with neutral effects, or provide the extra income that enables investment, such as purchasing a chainsaw or vehicle, that further accelerates resource loss? (Sutherland et al, 2004, p306)

Obviously any approach to conservation or development needs to be informed by evidence and, in that sense, the call for an evidence-based approach makes good sense. But there are difficulties inherent in assuming that there is a single clear and consistent answer to the question of whether 'clarifying who owns the property rights to each area results in long-term sustainable development or overexploitation'. The answer will almost certainly be 'yes' in some cases, 'no' in other cases and in most cases will depend on a whole range of additional situational and contextual factors. Causality can be highly complex and uncertain. Further, it is not predestined; a change in contextual factors (such as institutional arrangements at various levels) can lead to very different outcomes.[12]

It is also important to address the point that socio-economic approaches 'seem based upon faith and a political agenda rather than on the benefits to biodiversity'. This is not surprising. The rationale for addressing socio-economic factors is, at least to some extent, explicitly based on political (social justice) objectives. It is not based solely on assertions of benefits to biodiversity.

This book is based on the belief that conservation can do more to address poverty reduction and that poor ecosystem health will often undermine social and economic stability and the livelihoods of the poor. It should be clearly understood from the outset that this book is not advocating that poverty reduction is essential to biodiversity conservation.

Efforts at integrating conservation and development have sometimes been based on unrealistic assumptions about achieving win–win solutions. Obviously these are not always possible and it may be more realistic to look for trade-offs that may provide the best realistically possible outcomes. But, while assumptions about perfect solutions may be overly optimistic, it should not be thought that poverty reduction and conservation will always be in conflict. As the cases of Pred Nai and Shinyanga show (Chapter 3), rural people, and especially the poor, may have very good reasons for supporting the restoration of biodiversity in areas where severe degradation has occurred, providing appropriate institutional arrangements can be established. Restoring degraded lands provides considerable opportunities for improving conservation and poverty reduction.

Addressing poverty and conservation

The discussion about the links between livelihoods, poverty and conservation is not particularly new. Many conservationists have expressed concern about the need to take livelihoods and poverty into account in conservation activities. Since the 1970s, the movements advocating integrated conservation and development projects (ICDPs) and community-based conservation and resource management have reflected these concerns. Despite innovative and exciting work, however, ICDPs have been criticized for a lack of a clear framework and for weak or piecemeal implementation (McShane and Wells, 2004). In recent years, with the development of the livelihoods framework by the UK governments' Department for International Development (DFID) and other agencies,[13] terms such as 'pro-poor wildlife conservation' and 'pro-poor conservation' have appeared in conservation literature (DFID, 2002).[14] This book is not an attempt to replace these earlier approaches. Instead we stress the importance of commitment to poverty reduction within conservation activities.

As part of the concern with poverty reduction in conservation, human rights and social justice have emerged as fundamental issues. The rights of indigenous peoples to natural resources, especially in protected areas, have been recognized for many years and are encapsulated in a number of publications and policy statements (WWF, 1996; Beltrán, 2000; MacKay, 2002).

Others have advocated a stronger 'rights-based approach' to conservation, arguing that all conservation should start with a concern for human rights and, by implication, that this should be a primary concern of conservation. This book does not assert that human rights should necessarily be the primary concern of conservation. It does assert that, while conservation is justifiable on its own account, conservation approaches should also be socially just in the sense that they avoid or mitigate the 'actual [i.e. financial] and opportunity costs' of conservation to the poor (Phil Franks, CARE, personal communication). Social justice can be used as an operating principle, a measure to assess a minimum standard for conservation in areas where high levels of poverty persist. This can be thought of as a 'do not harm principle'. The minimum standard should be combined with a strong ethical commitment to support poverty reduction as a fundamental human right and development goal.

Discussion of 'rights' in conservation often revolves around the concept of environmental rights, understood as the right to a safe and healthy environment. This is often limited, in practice, to a concern for rights such as the right to clean water and the right to enjoy an aesthetically pleasing environment. It is more relevant, in the context of poverty reduction, to think in terms of more fundamental rights, such as the right to food, the right to shelter, the right to health, the right to enjoy cultural identity (a right which is particularly relevant to many indigenous peoples) and even the 'right to development', which is recognized in several international legal documents (Scanlon et al, 2004).

Cultural and indigenous issues are important in discussions of poverty and environment, partly because indigenous peoples are often especially vulnerable to environmental change and loss of environmental rights, partly because cultural identity is itself often linked to particular environments and partly because people who lose cultural identity are more prone to fall into poverty.

The conservation approach advocated in this book does not attempt to limit conservation activities to cases where poverty can be directly addressed. We are not proposing that conservation agencies stop worrying about conservation or that they become development-focused agencies. Rather, this book provides a broad approach for exploring negotiated outcomes in different types of circumstances, so that both conservation and land-use related development efforts are guided by social justice principles. Further, conservation should proactively look for opportunities to address poverty and livelihoods while development activities should actively support improved environmental management wherever possible. This is not about diluting the impact of conservation activities or shifting focus by stealth. Rather, it is about finding more appropriate, more equitable and more realistic ways of achieving conservation. We aim to augment the conservation tool kit by suggesting ways in which conservation can better address its associated social responsibilities.

Taking poverty reduction more seriously in conservation has a number of implications:

- All conservation initiatives should strive to ensure that they do not make the poor worse off. The costs of conservation should not be imposed on those least able to absorb them; they should be met by those groups – usually national governments and the international community – who regard conservation as a priority. This must go beyond narrow quid pro quo compensation. Best-practice measures designed to offset the impact of conservation activities should maintain, if not expand, development options, rather than leaving people in a poverty trap or a condition of 'sustainable poverty'.
- Conservation ought to contribute actively to poverty reduction more broadly where it can – as in the restoration of ecosystems – simply because it can.
- There is a pressing need to be more realistic. Integrated conservation and development may not result in perfect solutions, but an equitably balanced trade-off will still lead to better conservation outcomes than could have been achieved otherwise.
- Strengthening or guaranteeing access to natural resources will contribute to secure livelihoods for the people who depend on them. This implies that rural people will have more decentralized control over the resources that they have traditionally used and managed.

If conservationists and development specialists are serious about linking poverty reduction and conservation, then we must be able to show this in our performance. In other words, we must be accountable. This means that monitoring and evaluation of all conservation activities needs to take account of social impact assessment, particularly the impacts of activities on poor people. In cases where programmes or projects aim to maintain or improve livelihoods, or to increase income directly, methodologies must directly assess impacts in terms of costs and benefits to the poor.

Conclusions

There is an ethical imperative for conservation to take account of poverty issues. There are often good practical reasons for doing so. The issue is not promoting poverty reduction over conservation, but acknowledging that both poverty reduction and conservation are important objectives. It is often necessary to address both in order to achieve either. We want to avoid the stale argument about whether conservation is the means to achieve poverty reduction, or poverty reduction is the means to achieve conservation. Both are desirable objectives.

In practice, different actors will have different points of entry. Development practitioners may focus on reducing poverty, although conservation will often be necessary in order to achieve their objective. For conservationists, reducing threats to biodiversity may be paramount. Poverty reduction will be important as both an ethical prerequisite and as a practical requirement to achieve that objective.

This book is not offering a magic formula for conservation and development; on the contrary. Trade-offs will sometimes define the best possible (however imperfect) outcome. At the same time, attempts to balance economic development and conservation will often lead to better outcomes than would otherwise occur.

This book discusses several strategies for dealing jointly with poverty and conservation:

- focus on removing limitations (particularly institutional constraints) and building opportunities;
- identify causes of environmental degradation and poverty beyond the site level and address problems at appropriate levels, both geographically and institutionally;
- use landscape-based initiatives as well as – in many cases instead of – site-based solutions. This involves seeking ways to meet objectives in different parts of the wider landscape rather than trying to address all goals in a single site (such as a protected area).

Sustainable development needs negotiated outcomes that are equitable, economically viable and socially sustainable. It is easier to achieve this type of outcome at broader geographical scales rather than at the site level.

Notes

1   Sustainable development was defined by the World Commission on Environment and Development as 'development that meets the needs of the present without compromising the ability of future generations to meet their own needs' (WCED, 1987). An alternative definition is: 'improving the quality of human life while living within the carrying capacity of supporting ecosystems' (IUCN/UNEP/WWF, 1991). These two definitions are essentially compatible.

2   For a detailed discussion of issues relating to the MDGs and conservation see Roe (2004).

3   www.worldbank.org/poverty/mission/up3.htm

4   www.developmentgoals.org

5   www.iucn.org/themes/spg/portal/policy/mdg/mdg.htm

6   The relationship between poverty reduction (or 'poverty alleviation') has been the subject of debate in the pages of the journal *Oryx* (2003 and 2004). Sanderson and Redford (2003) argued that the emphasis on 'poverty alleviation' has largely replaced biodiversity conservation, but they acknowledge the importance of conservation to poverty alleviation. They worry that the costs of development (in the form of poverty alleviation) will again be borne by conservation. Roe and Elliott (2004) respond that 'poor people should not pay the price for biodiversity conservation'.

7   For a detailed discussion of the question of whether forests are safety nets or poverty traps, see Angelsen and Wunder (2003).

8   The text for the case study on Waza Logone was provided by Jean-Yves Pirot (IUCN).

9   It is important to stress here that the problem is forced resettlement. Voluntary resettlement or migration can be options for poverty reduction and many people have voluntarily chosen relocation as a strategy for improving their livelihoods.

10 At the fifth IUCN World Parks Congress in Durban, 8–17 September 2003, there was a strong recognition that conservation needs to take much more notice of the negative impacts of protected areas on the poor, as well as their potential to make a real contribution to poverty reduction through conservation activities (WPC Recommendation 29). For a discussion of ways in which protected areas can address poverty, see Scherl et al (2004).

11 We do not intend to discuss the literature on these asserted causal relationships in detail (we think our readers will recognize each of them). Examples in the following pages will illustrate the complexities of causal relationships in particular cases. For those who wish to explore the issue further, Angelsen and Kaimowitz (1999) review the literature about the causes of

deforestation, finding that there are 'serious questions concerning the conventional wisdom, either [... because of] contrary evidence or... the weakness of the supporting evidence' (p91).

12 Applying adaptive management is one way to deal with complex management issues without being paralysed by uncertainty and complexity. This approach proposes that actions be performed in situations where results are uncertain and then be modified based on careful monitoring of outcomes. (For a discussion of adaptive management applied to conservation, see Buck et al, 2001. For adaptive management of forests, see Fisher et al, 2007).

13 Oxfam, CARE and the United Nations Development Programme (UNDP) have all been actively involved in developing livelihoods-based approaches.

14 Although the term 'pro-poor' has frequently been applied to conservation approaches in the last few years, there are some serious difficulties with it. Perhaps the main concern is that it can sound paternalistic; it also has welfarist connotations (doing good for others). The intention in this book has been to avoid using any particular new term to describe the approach. It seems desirable to avoid developing a new term anyhow, as approaches with new names quickly become reduced to acronyms and the point gets lost.

2

Past Experiences

Introduction

This chapter provides essential background for the rest of the book. It begins with a brief review of previous experiences in dealing with people and conservation and outlines some of the key lessons learned from these experiences. It then turns to a discussion of poverty and livelihoods, followed by a look at some of the other ideas that have influenced the thinking. We want to emphasize that we are talking about 'people and conservation' in this chapter, not 'poverty and conservation', because many of the relevant experiences were not dealing explicitly with poverty.

This review of previous experiences aims to provide an overview of the important shifts in understanding of natural resource management practices during the last 50 years within the international conservation movement. In particular it explores the ways in which conservation thinking has developed and been influenced by sustainable development thinking. This not only helps to acknowledge the past social inadequacies of conservation, but also distinguishes a focus on poverty reduction from that of earlier traditions within conservation.

One of the difficulties in summarizing the major shift in conservation thinking, particularly as it pertains to local peoples, is that such shifts are never absolute. There are many contradictory movements and trends. We have attempted to nuance the discussion, while still highlighting key trends.

Reviewing past experiences[1]

1960s and 1970s: Nature as wilderness – people as threat

How was nature perceived in the early conservation literature in the 1960s and

1970s? And what were the perceived threats to this nature?

In the 1960s and 1970s, nature was often prized as a spiritually charged wilderness and for its capacity to uplift the human spirit. Such values, particularly when championed by social elite from both developed and developing countries, helped to shape the preservationist approach to nature and led to the establishment of parks to protect nature from the 'ravages of ordinary use' or the 'meddling hand of man'. It is important to recognize that assumptions about the 'natural' state of an ecosystem can be biased by prejudices about the destructiveness and ignorance of human populations and by spiritual beliefs about the value of wilderness.

The 'meddling hand of man' often referred to indigenous and other rural peoples living in and around wilderness. Ironically, much of the early concern with conservation in Africa came from non-native hunters who were members of the colonial elite and who saw no contradiction between their hunting activities and conservation. At the same time they perceived long-resident 'natives' as somehow separate from nature and intrinsically destructive (Adams and McShane, 1992). The landscape for safari hunting was seen as natural, but a landscape with resident populations was not. Adams and McShane (1992) show how some of these assumptions underlay the colonial origins of conservationist beliefs about 'wild Africa'.

Early conservation documents were not entirely anti-people, nor anti-use. Many documents saw conservation in the context of human use and described nature in use-value terms. *The Launching of a New Ark* stated: 'The Fund's campaign is not a case of animals versus man. Conservation is *for* man, and for the long-term benefit of humanity' (WWF, 1965, p23, original emphasis).

This conservation literature is replete with phrases justifying conservation 'in the name of all people', for 'common human interests' and 'for the benefit and enjoyment of all'. Arguably, such concepts help provide the basis for today's people-oriented approaches to conservation and sustainable use of resources. These documents were often more interesting for what they did not say. The universal moral arguments they put forward obscured the plurality of competing interests over nature and avoided the difficult politics of who benefited and who decided. While conservation agencies liked to portray themselves as 'trustees for all generations', there was little self-reflection on their moral authority, if any, to establish and manage protected areas. Appeals for conservation were rarely made on behalf of poor resource users, and access to national parks demanded social privileges. In short, the approach was undoubtedly elitist and very much favoured the value of nature to humans in general (as defined by an elite view). There was little interest in the value of nature to poor rural people.

Combined with the prevailing theories of environmental degradation, such elitist perspectives seriously undermined the interests of many rural resource users. As McCormick (1995) pointed out, the perception of the relationships between local people and nature was influenced by the environmentalism of the so-called

'Prophets of Doom'. Threats to nature in developing countries were usually framed in terms of the 'ignorant behaviour' and 'reckless management' of rural peoples and in the context of 'uncontrolled population growth', referred to in one case as 'senseless multiplication' (Nicholson, 1981). The problems identified with these threats included overgrazing and exceeding the land's carrying capacity, slash-and-burn agriculture, the impoverishment of vegetation leading to the disappearance of climax vegetation, as well as the poaching of wildlife.

Solutions for protecting nature inevitably followed. In the early years conservation funds financed preservationist approaches to conservation, such as establishing protected areas and reserves, removing local populations, supplying anti-poaching equipment and conducting animal and plant surveys. The perception of rural people as threats to the environment supported efforts to remove them from protected areas and underpinned many early education programmes that sought to improve attitudes and 'primitive' practices. Early preservationist approaches adopted militaristic tactics and infrastructure, described by later critics as 'fortress' conservation, along with its 'fines and fences' approach.

In many cases, the establishment of protected areas failed to consider the social costs, including gross violations of human rights and the economic and political marginalization of thousands of rural people (Turnbull, 1974; Colchester, 1994; Ghimire and Pimbert, 1997). Several analysts have recognized that the very language of these early conservation efforts affects the way we think about people living in or around protected areas. Local people were – and still are – labelled as 'poachers' or 'squatters' rather than 'hunters' or 'settlers' (Brown, 1991; Colchester, 1994).

Exclusionary approaches had several effects on rural resource users:

- forced (sometimes violent) resettlement of local populations;
- prohibited or restricted access to livelihood resources;
- break-up of communal lands;
- collapse of indigenous management systems and social structures;
- fines and imprisonment;
- increased rural conflict and famine.

Although the fortress perspective dominated this period, it was not the only interpretation of conservation. The early conservation movement was not exclusively anti-local people, nor totally unconcerned about livelihoods. A 1961 conference[2] discussed the needs of local people and their attitudes to nature. It was noted that wildlife management outside and adjacent to national parks depended on the needs, way of life and cooperation of local communities. The point was made that preservation alone was not the answer and that emphasis should be given to 'using' wildlife (Hillaby, 1961).

By the mid-1970s, Raymond Dasmann, a senior IUCN ecologist, was writing extensively about the injustices of protected areas. He developed a set of principles that he considered mandatory for agencies responsible for creating new national parks. These principles anticipated many of the developments addressed in the conservation literature of the 1990s, including rights of ownership, tenure and resource use, use of local knowledge, local involvement in planning and management, protection of native cultures, sharing economic benefits with local peoples, recognition of different social interests and development of surrounding areas (Dasmann, 1976, pp166–167; 1984, pp670–671).

The principles did not, however, include allowing local people to share the land with the animals in and around protected areas (Adams and McShane, 1992). That concept was eclipsed by preservationist values and supported by prevailing ecological theories.

Early conservation practices have been critiqued on many grounds:

- they were ethnocentric, favouring Western ideas of nature;
- they were elitist, failing to consider the land rights and sophisticated resource management of indigenous inhabitants;
- they were based on outmoded ecological models that 'freeze' the ecological status quo and ignore the dynamics of the wider and human-influenced landscapes of which ecosystems are ultimately a part;
- they were self-defeating – removing people from parks caused ecological simplification, and outside pressures eventually impinged on protected areas.

Nature as biodiversity – people as a resource

By the end of the 1970s, international conservation adopted various 'conservation with development' approaches, promoting the idea that conservation and development were interdependent. Such views are articulated by both the *World Conservation Strategy* (IUCN/UNEP/WWF, 1980) and *Caring for the Earth* (IUCN/UNEP/WWF, 1991). These reflected important changes in the understanding of the relationship between people and nature.

By the 1980s, many conservationists had begun to move away from earlier preoccupations with flagship species and special areas, and to question the underlying causes of environmental degradation. They adopted more strategic programmes that emphasized ecological processes and life-support systems. In this context, 'nature' came to be represented more as 'biodiversity', 'biospheres' and 'ecosystems'. The loss of biodiversity developed into a central theme of conservation science.

The conservation and development literature of the 1980s recast people–nature relationships in two important ways. First, it was now increasingly accepted that it was neither ethically justifiable nor politically feasible to exclude poor people from parks without providing alternative livelihoods (Brandon and Wells, 1992), although this ethical and political imperative was often ignored in practice. Rural people were no longer blamed as the principal agents of environmental destruction, or if they were, more attention was paid to the poverty that was believed to force them into unsustainable practices. There was a shift from seeing rural people as ignorant instruments of environmental degradation to seeing them as unwilling instruments. As Carwardine (1990, p54) put it:

many of the people destroying rainforests can hardly be called villains. The landless peasants, desperate for a patch on which to grow their food, are really victims of other underlying problems, such as overpopulation and widespread poverty.

At the same time, other narratives began to extol the virtues of 'traditional people' who had lived for generations in 'harmony with nature'. New research began to reveal how indigenous and traditional peoples made important contributions to a global understanding of sustainable use and conservation (McNeely and Pitt, 1985; Posey, 1985; Kemf, 1993). Solutions to newly perceived problems focused on buffer zones around protected areas, sustainable utilization, ICDPs and forms of community-based natural resource management (CBNRM). Some of these are discussed in more detail below.

While the shift to integrated conservation and development was widely supported by international conservation organizations in the 1980s, it was not always accepted. To some organizations, tackling social concerns was only a means to an end – nature conservation. This was a standard view within conservation organizations during that time:

Conservation projects should be more people-oriented – but not people projects. Conservation organisations should always be looking for ways to ensure the long term success of their protected area projects by linking them with integrated conservation and development projects (ICDPs), but conservation organisations must remember that they are not development agencies. (Response in a WWF field staff survey, 1992)

According to Adams (1990), the conservation-with-development discourse constitutes a repackaging and not a radical redefinition. While local needs are acknowledged, and resource users are no longer represented as a direct threat to nature, local people tend to be recast as a 'resource' for achieving global conservation objectives as defined by scientific experts.

Integrated conservation and development projects

ICDPs attempt to combine biodiversity conservation with improvements in human wellbeing. They evolved as early as the 1960s in response to the failures of earlier conservation approaches and have been increasingly common since the 1980s. The first generation of ICDPs had three major approaches to reducing pressure on protected areas:

1   strengthening park management and creating buffer zones around protected areas;
2   providing compensation or substitution to local people for loss of access to resources;
3   encouraging local socio-economic development among communities adjacent to protected area boundaries.

Earlier ICDPs were usually concerned with providing alternatives to natural resource use in protected areas, not about sustainable use of resources in these areas.

ICDPs have been enormously attractive to national and international agencies, NGOs and donors involved in biodiversity conservation and sustainable development, although this is unlikely to continue indefinitely without concrete demonstrations of progress. Very few projects have been able to demonstrate significant improvements in either conservation or human wellbeing, and even fewer have contributed to both. Sceptics argue that the idea of integrated conservation and development is conceptually flawed and that most of the practical difficulties of ICDPs are generated by the unrealistic assumptions about this integration. There is some merit to this point. It is unrealistic to expect win–win solutions to all attempts to combine conservation and development. Trade-offs often need to be made, but synergies are also possible. The important thing is to aim for the best of all realistic outcomes through negotiation and also to ensure that outcomes are equitable in that they do impose costs on those least able to pay them.

Critiques of ICDPs have been framed in the context of the three pillars of sustainable development: biodiversity conservation, social development and economic opportunities.

Biodiversity conservation

Most ICDPs have no systematic programmes to monitor their effects on biodiversity, making it difficult to judge whether they are achieving their conservation goals. In fact, many ICDPs have had difficulty in establishing specific conservation targets, such as the extent of an ecosystem or the number of species to be conserved. This has made project interventions hard to evaluate. Ecologists have warned that some integrated conservation and development initiatives, based on the extraction and marketing of non-timber forest products (NTFPs), are unsound and that we simply do not know the ecological effects of harvesting particular species on the sustainability of the forest ecosystem as a whole. Other analysts point out that ICDPs may actually exacerbate ecological destruction by acting as growth magnets and encouraging people to migrate into project areas (Oates, 1999). In short, there is concern that ICDPs do not provide an effective strategy for conserving nature.

Some authors have gone further than this, arguing not only that ICDPs have not been able to provide an effective conservation strategy, but that they cannot do so.

Social development

Many ICDPs have been unsuccessful in achieving their social development goals and have demonstrated a serious lack of understanding of the social dimensions of conservation. Problems have arisen in understanding the dynamics of local communities and in facilitating public participation in ICDP project design, implementation and evaluation. Indigenous technical knowledge has not always been incorporated into programme activities and it has proved difficult to build on indigenous management institutions under rapidly changing conditions. Challenges include institution building and strengthening the internal capacity of rural organizations to make transparent, informed and consensual decisions. There have also been difficulties in working with multiple stakeholders with different interests and status, particularly given the intense pressure on landscapes from land clearing for agriculture, logging (sometimes illegal) and commercial enterprises, which are frequently supported by powerful economic and political interests. Poverty and social inequities within the vicinity of many ICDPs remain acute.

Economic opportunities

The economic benefits generated by ICDPs have not usually been enough – either as an incentive or an alternative – to prevent the activities that put pressure on protected areas. Few projects have been able to provide the range of income-generating, labour-intensive activities that satisfy the livelihood needs of local inhabitants. Benefits from project activities have not been distributed fairly; most benefits have been received by wealthier people rather than the poorest groups. Some new activities have come into conflict with peoples' livelihood strategies, such as hunting and gathering.

Until recently, most economic activities associated with ICDPs have occurred in areas adjacent to, but outside, protected areas, with the intent of allowing local people to essentially substitute for consumption or income from protected areas. More recent emphasis has been placed on sustainable use, both for consumption and income generation. The harvesting and marketing of NTFPs, and developing marketing strategies and systems for them, is especially relevant here.

Marketing NTFPs presents many problems. Some products have low market values or volatile prices. Unless the size of a market can be increased, assisting some people to gain income from NTFPs may do no more than change the way the cake is shared, without increasing the size of the cake. Difficulties arise from fragmented markets, from market saturation with particular products (thus decreasing prices) and from inadequate processing equipment and physical infrastructure. Lack of access to credit can limit the development of new enterprises; substantial subsidies have often been required to develop viable enterprises.

Although ecotourism provides another potential economic opportunity, ecotourism ventures have often been overrated as a way of reducing poverty around protected areas, especially in areas with social instability and national insecurity. Providing compensation for conservation has proved impractical in some cases due to the support required for local communities and the costs of protected area management over the long term.

Managing ICDPs

ICDPs have been implemented on a very small scale, with little financial support, inadequate technical skills and insufficient political backing. Project staff have been few in number, spread thinly over large geographical areas, and have lacked the technical skills, capacities and knowledge to work on social issues or with a wide variety of interest groups. Many ICDPs have been set up as development projects and government responsibilities for law enforcement have been neglected. Few park agencies have had jurisdiction outside park boundaries; most have lacked the authority to regulate buffer zone activities in the absence of legislative changes.

It is widely recognized that the broader policy environment has an enormous influence on project effectiveness and that external (non-local) forces often drive conservation and development issues. Unless national political frameworks support project initiatives, particularly devolution of power to the local level, locally based management is unlikely to succeed.

In addition, ICDPs need long-term commitment and reliable funding. They are not suitable for the typical three- to five-year project cycle approach where continuity cannot be assured. While projects may be useful as policy experiments (see Chapter 5), they can only be successful in the long term with appropriate supporting policy and legislative frameworks and if their approach becomes part of a more comprehensive programme.

ICDPs: Flawed in theory?

Some conservationists have argued that the basic idea of integrated conservation and development is flawed. Oates (1999), in a strong attack on ICDPs, argues that integrated conservation and development has not worked for conservation (especially biodiversity conservation) and that there are fundamental flaws in the theory that wildlife can best be conserved through human economic development. He describes this theory as a myth. (This can be interpreted in the anthropological sense of a myth of charter, or a myth that justifies a certain course of behaviour or action, not just the more popular sense of a widely believed untruth. Oates seems to intend both meanings.)

Oates argues that there is another myth: traditional peoples are natural conservationists. But, balancing this is another opposing myth that suggests that traditional people are natural opponents of nature and biodiversity.[3] This illustrates a serious problem with much of the discussion about people and conservation – the tendency for the sort of argument that says that people are essentially one thing or another and always behave in a certain way. The problem with such an argument is that it fails to account for context. Behaviour, whether conservationist or exploitative, always occurs in the context of complex social, economic and environmental circumstances.

In arguing that integrated conservation and development can be counterproductive, Oates suggests that people may move into areas of high-priority conservation in order to obtain economic benefits, thus increasing the pressure on the remaining natural resources. Although this sounds plausible and similar arguments are often made, there is remarkably little evidence that this actually does occur, apart from cases where a national park attracts people to work in the tourism industry.[4] In such cases it is not an integrated project that attracts outside pressure, but the economic opportunities associated with nature tourism and it is, generally, the economically well-off who are attracted to such opportunities rather than the poor. In any case, given that Oates himself says that integrated projects produce few benefits for local communities, it is hard to see why the absence of benefits would attract additional population and pressure on resources.

Oates points out that the concept of sustainable development ignores the intrinsic value of nature by focusing entirely on its use value. This is a legitimate point but, given that some peoples' livelihoods are severely damaged by conservation activities, it seems necessary to ask who should decide whether use values or intrinsic values are more important.

Oates argues strongly against the common view that conservation can only work with peoples' cooperation. He claims that there are cases where it can work, despite views to the contrary, and presents evidence of successful 'traditional' conservation (in terms of conservation outcomes). Indeed, Brockington (2003) makes the same point about successful 'traditional' conservation with reference to the Mkomazi Game Reserve in northeast Tanzania. However, Brockington's conclusion is dramatically different. His point is that it was possible to achieve conservation objectives without local support, but only at the cost of local peoples' livelihoods and wellbeing. He argues that such conservation is unethical, even if traditional exclusionary approaches are feasible in terms of conservation.

In addition to the ethical issues involved, there are practical reasons, from a conservation point of view, for questioning conservation approaches that use coercion, often supported by police or military power, to exclude local people who depend on natural resources. It is doubtful that a 'conservation in a vacuum' approach could be economically sustainable in the long term, given the financial costs of policing and coercion. The political costs are also likely to be increasingly difficult to sustain.

Just as it is a mistake to overemphasize the potential for win–win solutions to conservation and development, it is also possible to exaggerate the extent to which conservation and development are in conflict. There are many cases where conflict between objectives is not an issue.

The question of combining conservation and development is not just whether it works. For ethical reasons it must be made to work. The question is how.

New-generation ICDPs

Despite the failures reported above, some analysts argue that ICDPs can still be successful with learning and modification. Wells et al (2004) argue that future ICDPs need to be designed on the basis of clearly defined objectives and that they must have explicit targets and testable assumptions. They need to be implemented through decentralized and adaptive management that is based on specific local conditions and local community dynamics, and they must be more proactive in addressing diverse stakeholder interests. ICDPs must also be part of a vertically integrated mix of site-based programmes and policy initiatives in order to address multiple-scale problems beyond the range of local solutions.

Collaborative management

Over the last ten years, collaborative management of protected areas has been a trend in ICDPs (Borrini-Feyerabend, 1997). It has also been applied to conservation outside protected areas, especially in forestry (see Fisher (1995) for an overview of collaborative management in forestry). Collaborative management involves a partnership between stakeholders, especially protected area authorities and local communities. Collaborative management is not discussed in detail here, but much of the discussion of community-based conservation in the next section applies to it.

Positive aspects of protected areas

Much of the previous discussion has been critical of the impacts of protected areas on the poor and especially critical of the failure of protected area management to seriously address the needs of poor people living in and around them or the negative impacts of protection on the poor. These are major criticisms. However, we should stress that protected areas can make positive contributions to the poor.

Protected areas often have a critical role in conserving ecosystem functionality through protecting watersheds and this has importance to the rural poor. In some cases (as in Central America), protected areas can play an important part in protecting ecosystems that are ecologically vulnerable and critical to the poor (such as mangroves, coastal forests and watersheds). It is notable that local people sometimes seek to have protected areas declared in order to protect resources more effectively. One example of this is the case of artisanal fisherman on Qeshm Island in the Persian Gulf who sought to have offshore fisheries declared a 'marine protected area' in order to prevent damage by large-scale commercial fishing.[5] A crucial point in this case was the expectation that declaration of a protected area would not prevent artisanal fishing.

Recent initiatives in protected area policy are in the direction of increasing benefits for the poor and addressing poverty. Nevertheless, much protected area management practice continues to pay limited attention to the rights and needs of resident people. An approach based on 'do no harm' principles, secure livelihoods, secure rights and increased benefits from protected area activity is evolving but has yet to be widely applied.

Community-based conservation

ICDPs have mainly been applied to protected areas and to buffer zones associated with them. As noted in Chapter 1, meaningful conservation cannot be achieved by focusing on protected areas alone, and opportunities for partnerships between conservation and poverty reduction are considerable outside protected areas. There are many cases outside protected areas – and, less frequently, within protected areas – where communities have attempted to integrate conservation and development.

Community-based conservation, sometimes known as CBNRM, consists of a wide variety of initiatives. The term loosely encompasses a number of other concepts, including community forestry, collaborative forest management and community fisheries. Western and Wright (1994, p9) argue that its central precept is 'the co-existence of people and nature, as distinct from protectionism and the segregation of people and nature' and that it is essentially about 'the locus of action'.

This last point is important. Critics of community-based conservation often complain that supporters naively assume that communities are homogeneous and that this assumption leads to unrealistic expectations of cooperation. This is an inaccurate claim. In fact, many advocates of CBNRM stress the heterogeneity of communities and the potential for conflicts over resource use,[6] but they also argue that heterogeneity is not an excuse for ignoring the potential of CBNRM, that conflicts can be and must be managed (just as they must be at any level of society) and that developing institutional mechanisms to deal with conflict should be a major focus of intervention. Advocating CBNRM does not assume

---

Box 2.1 Human actions and biodiversity

It has often been assumed that any human use of resources upsets the equilibrium and that human activities must inevitably lead to environmental degradation. Research shows, however, that under some conditions, human action can actually lead to increased biodiversity. For example, Fairhead and Leach (1996) examine what they call the savanna-forest mosaic south of the West African Sahel. This environment consists of large areas of savanna with scattered forest patches. The normally accepted view, from the early colonial period until the recent past, was that the agricultural practices of the human population had, through burning and other practices, led to the degradation of what was originally forest into the current savanna. However, Fairhead and Leach demonstrated, through comparison of aerial photographs from the 1950s and recent satellite imagery, that the number of forest patches was increasing and that this was occurring around settlements. Complementing this comparison with ethnographic research (including oral history), they concluded that the savanna was natural and that human activities, far from destroying forest, had actually contributed to an increase in tree cover and the development of a mosaic of forest niches. In other words, disturbances resulting from human activities increased biodiversity rather than reducing it.

---

that communities are homogeneous, it merely states that natural resource management needs to be associated with a locally resident population[7] rather than with remote authorities.

In the conservation literature, CBNRM is often distinguished from top-down conservation approaches:

> *Community-based conservation reverses the top down, center driven conservation by focussing on the people who bear the costs of conservation. In the broadest sense then, community-based conservation includes natural resources or biodiversity protection by, for and with the local community. (Western and Wright, 1994, p7)*

The move towards community-based approaches to conservation and resource management has been influenced by a number of factors:

- There has been an increasing recognition that, rather than destroying nature, local people have actually enriched biodiversity and landscapes in many areas (Posey, 1985; Gilmour and Fisher, 1991; Gomez-Pompa and Kaus, 1992; Fairhead and Leach, 1995, 1998; Pimbert and Pretty, 1995; Poffenberger and McGean, 1996). Although conservation theory in past years declared that nature could be protected only by removing people, more recent research has demonstrated that the absence of local management may actually cause biological simplification in some areas (Chase, 1987; Adams and McShane, 1992; Western and Giochio, 1993; Pimbert and Gujja, 1997).
- This has been associated with an increased understanding of how indigenous

institutions and indigenous knowledge help maintain relatively stable environmental conditions over long periods of time (see, for example, Kunstadter et al, 1978; Fisher, 1989).

It is obvious that the discourse on local and indigenous knowledge and local and indigenous organizations and institutions can be romanticized. Certainly, local and indigenous resource management systems are not perfect. They are often flawed or ineffective, even absent. (The same can be said, of course, for science-based management by state authorities.) The problem is to maintain a balance between demonizing the practices of local people in relation to the environment and romanticizing them. The reality is that sustainable management and degradation both occur as a result of the activities of local people, as do all sorts of outcomes along the continuum.

This has implications for conservation practice. The emphasis shifts from asking whether local management systems work (as if there was a single universal answer to that question), to asking why they work in some cases and not in others. Arrangements can be strengthened where they are present, and developed where they are not. The extensive literature on the management of common property resources provides useful insights into why some local institutional arrangements work and some do not (see, for example, Ostrom (1990) and the literature arising from conferences sponsored by the International Association for the Study of Common Property).

• The assumption that population growth leads inevitably to land degradation and deforestation has increasingly been questioned by research (Blaikie and Brookfield, 1987; Colchester and Lohmann, 1993). Forest cover and diversity can actually increase in some areas as population density increases because there are greater incentives to use resources more efficiently (Tiffen et al, 1994; Sayer, 1995; see also Box 2.1). Shinyanga (Chapter 3) is one clear example of environmental conditions improving despite a population increase. While many of these examples do not necessarily imply new conservation approaches, they do provide a new context within which rural peoples' activities can be better appreciated, thus lending support to community-based conservation approaches.

• Community-based conservation has also been influenced by the human rights and indigenous peoples' movement. These view human rights, social justice and livelihoods, rather than nature, as the top priority. Such perspectives are often rooted in histories of popular resistance to government appropriation of land, where the motivation for conservation stems from alarm at the devastating effects of globalization on the lives of poor and politically marginalized rural communities, including indigenous peoples (Guha, 1989; Lohmann, 1991; Colchester, 1992, 1994; IWGIA, 1996; Peet and Watts, 1996; Guha and Martinez-Alier, 1997).

An enormous variety of community-based conservation and resource management systems exist throughout the world. It is often difficult to assess them, partly due to inconsistent terminology. A plethora of terms like community-based conservation, CBNRM, community forestry, community-based forestry and ICDPs are used in different and often contradictory ways.

Fisher (1989) distinguishes between indigenous forest management systems and sponsored systems, defined by whether the initiative for establishing local forest management systems arose from local people or from outsiders, such as government agencies. This distinction can also be applied to any local (community-based) conservation or natural resource management systems. These, of course, are broad types. In practice, specific community-based arrangements may have been initiated through a combination of local and external initiatives.

Community-based arrangements can also be classified in terms of tenure (the arrangements governing access to resources) and the related power to make decisions about resources. Tenure and decision-making power are important factors in successful CBNRM. (This is discussed more in Chapter 5.)

Finally, community-based arrangements can be classified in terms of the nature of the relationship between the community institution and government agencies and other external actors. This may range from virtual independence through some sort of joint management or power sharing through to dominance by an outside agency.

Barrow et al (2000) have compared a number of different types of community conservation according to a variety of factors, including tenure (Table 2.1). They distinguish between three broad types of arrangements involving communities and reflecting relationships with government agencies, especially conservation agencies: Protected area outreach, collaborative management and community-based conservation. Although their analysis is based on experiences from Africa, and the terminology may differ, the broad types are recognizable more widely.

Table 2.1 *Components of community conservation*

Component	Protected area outreach	Collaborative management	Community-based conservation
Whose agenda	Dominantly protected area in having neighbours as partners	Dominantly protected area, going to joint	Community, local level
Who owns process	Protected area	Legally the state, but towards joint management	Community
Who plans	For outreach activities can be joint	Joint	Community, often with assistance of others

Who controls	Protected area	Joint	Community
Ownership of resources, area	Protected area	Protected area	De facto community, or individual, but will depend on how tenure is vested
Dominant objective	Enhanced conservation	Conservation with increased access and use	Rural livelihoods: needs met but conservation values integrated
Fate of conservation resource	Maintained, as part of states' conservation heritage	Maintained, as part of states' conservation heritage; however may be overuse, or use may affect other species	Where insignificant to rural economics or culture, resource will be lost; resource likely to be maintained the more culturally and economically valuable it is
Value of local rules and regulations	Slight, related to how positive the relationship is	Can be great depending on how local rules of access join with park rules and who enforces	Local rules will govern access and use of resources, by whom and under what conditions
Influence of increased population	Reduced value of outreach as benefits shared more thinly. Increased need for park integrity maintenance	Pressures on how many different stakeholders can have access to a relatively static resource; how community handles inclusion and exclusion is key	Since conservation resource base not likely to increase, benefits spread more thinly and value per person may decrease; how community handles inclusion and exclusion is key
Community role in conservation	Conservation for or with the people	Conservation with or by the people	Conservation by the people

Source: Slightly modified from Barrow et al (2000)

Sustainable use in CBNRM

CBNRM, especially where it is externally sponsored, has not always focused on sustainable use. In Nepal, with its established and well-supported community forestry programme, community forestry still tends to be very conservative in terms of use, focusing mostly on products such as fuelwood for domestic use and NTFPs for domestic use and sale. Although there have been some experiments in commercial harvesting of forests and timber processing by community forestry user groups (see, for example, Jackson and Ingles, 1994), these have been relatively scarce and have received limited official recognition and support.

Some significant experiments with sustainable use of wildlife have taken place in Africa, especially the innovative, well-documented and increasingly imitated

CAMPFIRE (Communal Areas Management Programme for Indigenous Resources) programme in Zimbabwe (see Box 2.2). There has been a great deal of discussion of sustainable wildlife management, especially in Africa (for an overview see Hulme and Murphree, 2001).

Box 2.2 CAMPFIRE, Zimbabwe

Economic incentives are central to CAMPFIRE. In Zimbabwe, six of the 16 primary wildlife districts are among the country's least developed. Most of them are located at the margins of the country, next to protected areas, and in agriculturally marginal areas. CAMPFIRE depends mostly on the sport-hunting industry and is based on the rights to use wildlife, which are leased to a private sector entrepreneur by the Rural District Council. The devolution of appropriate authority from the central government to the district level has resulted in the greater use of market-based mechanisms for the allocation of leases and greater efficiency of resource use. A significant amount of revenue is devolved to the ward (village or community) level and provides the financial incentives for individual and households to participate in the common management of wildlife. In addition, some rural people are employed by the sport-hunting companies, or provide goods. The wards then use the income for various activities, such as school buildings, clinics and cereal-grinding mills. In some cases there are cash dividends for individual farmers.

Between 1989 and 1996, the revenue earned and retained by rural district councils with appropriate authority exceeded US$9.3 million, more than 90 per cent of which came from sport hunting. Of this income, 53 per cent was disbursed to the ward level and 22 per cent was used for wildlife and programme management, while the council levied 13 per cent and the remaining 12 per cent was allocated for other uses. The returns per household declined from US$19.40 in 1989 to US$4.49 in 1996, primarily due to the decreasing wildlife production potential in the growing number of wards participating in CAMPFIRE. The income from the CAMPFIRE programme averaged 17 per cent of gross agricultural income, although after the severe drought of 1991 it rose to 21 per cent. Income from sport hunting is influenced by the numbers and variety of wildlife, which decrease as population density increases. In cases where wildlife is plentiful and human population densities are low, returns from sport hunting to rural people are much higher. It is clear that returns from sport hunting can contribute significantly to livelihood security, particularly in times of drought. But not all areas with wildlife have enough variety or numbers to sustain viable returns from wildlife to rural people, and other options need to be considered, such as photographic tourism and walking safaris. In addition weakened macro-economic performance poses a significant challenge to the future success of programmes such as CAMPFIRE.

Source: Slightly modified from Bond (2001)

Not all of the literature related to CBNRM has been positive. In an argument that is somewhat similar to that presented by Oates (1999, p27), Barrett and Arcese (1995) argue that attempts to link rural development and species conservation are flawed because they may increase dependence on game meat and therefore increase demand. They also argue that successful projects will probably lead to an increase in population growth, partly by attracting poor immigrants. In a strong response to this argument, Murphree (1996) points out that the argument is somewhat condescending, a point which is 'implied in the warnings about giving rural peoples a taste for meat or encouraging them to enter markets where they will be diddled'(p160). But he also points out that Barrett and Arcese assume that projects of this type are essentially concerned with people living around protected areas and that wildlife is essentially a product of protected areas. He points out that, in fact, 'wildlife and sustainable development is not primarily about parks/people relationships, although it may have some implications for these relationships' (Murphree, 1996, p161).

This is a very important point. It is a reminder that a great deal of community-based conservation occurs outside protected areas and that many of the most successful projects, in both conservation and rural development terms, occur in non-protected landscapes.

Has CBNRM contributed to poverty reduction?

While it is clear that community-based conservation activities can contribute to poverty reduction and sustainable livelihoods (see, for example, the cases of Shinyanga and Pred Nai in Chapter 3 and CAMPFIRE in Box 2.2), ICDPs generally have not been particularly successful in this respect. The benefits of externally sponsored forestry projects and programmes have been limited or at least poorly documented (Fisher, 2000). Claims of extensive benefits are often dubious, particularly in the case of project-based activities or government programmes.

In the case of community forestry in Nepal, there is no doubt that the government programme has contributed to improvements in forest conditions, or that it has involved many households. Malla (2000) has argued, however, that income generation for the poor has been limited. In fact, he argues that the poor are sometimes worse off than before. Joint Forest Management in India has also raised serious questions about equity and poverty reduction (see Sarin (1998), discussed further in Chapter 5).

There are more positive accounts. Gilmour et al (2004) report on the linkages between community forestry and poverty in Asia. (They are referring to official community forestry programmes rather than community-initiated activities.) They found that there was 'some clear empirical evidence through case studies, that community forestry has provided some tangible benefits to poor people. The evidence is, however, limited to a few cases and there is no clear evidence of scaling-up' (Gilmour et al, 2004, p1).

While positive examples do exist, it is important to ask why potentially promising programmes have had relatively limited success and why benefits have not been more widely distributed.[8] Failures often relate to questions of power and poor institutional arrangements, issues that are pursued in Chapter 5.

Lessons from CBNRM

There are some important lessons from the many examples of community-based initiatives:

- Secure access to natural resources is important both for food and for livelihood security (with important implications for conservation to address poverty reduction). Opinions differ as to whether secure access requires full legal ownership (see Chapter 5).
- Devolved decision-making authority is also important (again, see Chapter 5 for further discussion).
- Without secure access and genuinely devolved decision-making authority, CBNRM is unlikely to allow significant use of resources and will tend to ignore the interests of the poor.
- Community institutions in CBNRM can often be controlled by local elites and the interests of the poor are often ignored. This is especially likely when CBNRM is externally sponsored or controlled, since outside agencies tend to work with and support elites. Institutional development for CBNRM needs to be carefully crafted to meet the needs of the poor.

Implications of these changes

This chapter has explored how the views of people–nature relationships within international conservation agencies have transformed over the last 50 years. While people were seen as a principal 'threat to nature' during the 1960s, literature of the 1980s and 1990s tended to portray them as a 'resource for conservation'. Conservation has been criticized for using poverty reduction and sustainable livelihoods as a means of achieving conservation rather than as serious objectives in their own right. Alternatively, many development programmes have viewed conservation as a minor add-on and have failed to see sustainable use of resources as a necessary part of sustainable development.

There is increasing acknowledgment of the need to recognize 'rights to resources' as the basis of addressing poverty reduction. A great deal has been learned from ICDPs and other community-based approaches to conservation and development. The challenge for the future is to achieve better sustainable development, with a more serious commitment to the rights of the poor to development and with more substantive attempts to effectively link the three pillars of sustainable development.

Chapter 3 presents a number of case studies that better illustrate some of the linkages between conservation and society and that point to lessons from constructive interventions that can better support the linkages.

Some key concepts

The multiple dimensions of poverty

According to the World Bank (2004), in 2000 about 1.1 billion people (nearly one fifth of the world's population) lived in absolute poverty – subsisting on less than US$1 a day. There are many definitions of poverty and many strategies to solve it. Economists often use notions of 'absolute poverty' and 'the poverty line'. The poverty line is the level of per capita consumption that permits the individual to satisfy basic nutritional requirements. The notional poverty line of US$1 per day is a figure currently used to reflect a person's ability to afford a diet sufficient to meet minimal nutritional needs. Absolute poverty is defined as existing where income falls below this poverty line (World Bank, 2001). There are various technical difficulties in measuring poverty in these terms, and questions arise about what such measurements do not and cannot tell us. For example, while the measurement of absolute poverty may be able to reveal something about physical well-being, it cannot throw light on the underlying causes of poverty or the significance of power structures and processes in reproducing it (Hanmer et al, 1999). Nevertheless, in gross terms, the poverty line is a useful indicator.

Since the 1980s, a great deal of qualitative research has been done with rural people in low-income countries to help develop a much broader conceptual view of poverty and deprivation (Chambers, 1988; Narayan et al, 2000). Many such studies reveal the political, historical and psychological aspects of poverty, such as social exclusion and powerlessness, as well as material deprivation. Amartya Sen (1999, p87) has identified poverty as 'the deprivation of basic capabilities', which are 'the substantive freedoms [a person] enjoys to lead the kind of life he or she has reason to value' (p87). He focuses on deprivations that intrinsically limit peoples' freedoms, rather than low income, which he sees as significant only in the sense that it can be 'a principal reason for a person's capability deprivation'.

The emergence of a multidimensional view of poverty shifts the focus to issues such as power to make decisions and access to information. A multidimensional concept of poverty, incorporating both income and non-income elements, has recently been widely accepted. Many of the non-income dimensions of poverty are less amenable to measurement and tend to raise difficult questions about social inequalities and power and how to address them (Craig and Porter, 2003).

This book applies the World Bank's concept of poverty (World Bank, 2001). This avoids the narrow definition of a lack of income and, according to Maxwell (2003), is the closest yet to an international consensus on how to understand poverty and how to reduce it. According to the World Bank view there are three dimensions of poverty: lack of assets, powerlessness and vulnerability. These are outlined in Table 2.2.

Table 2.2 *Dimensions of poverty*

Lack of assets	Powerlessness	Vulnerability
Assets include: • natural capital • human capital • financial capital • physical capital • social capital	Powerlessness caused by: • social differences (including gender) • inequitable access to resources • unresponsive public administrations • corruption • inequitable legal systems	Multiple risks resulting from: • economic crises • natural disasters • social crises

Source: Adapted from World Bank (2001)

Based on this analysis, the World Bank promotes a three-pronged strategy for poverty reduction: building assets by providing opportunities for growth, empowerment and increasing security. Some examples of these strategies are outlined in Table 2.3.

Table 2.3 *Some dimensions of poverty reduction*

Opportunities and growth	Empowerment	Security
• expanding assets of poor • encouraging private investments • expanding international markets • pro-poor market reform • restructuring aid • debt relief	• addressing social inequalities • enhanced public participation in decision making • pro-poor decentralization • public administration reform • legal reform • providing forums for debate	• risk management • safety nets • coping with natural disasters

Disaggregating social categories

Understanding the impacts of policies and developmental activities on the poor requires efforts to disaggregate social categories. Simply adding up net benefits misses the impact that particular actions can have on different categories of people. For this reason, taking poverty seriously in conservation requires recognition of the different effects of actions, both positive and negative, on different groups of people.

Since the 1970s much of the focus of social science research on people and the environment has shifted to concepts of 'social difference' (Leach et al, 1997). Such concepts have served to undermine simplistic notions of 'the local community' as a homogeneous and static whole. Rather than studying functional adaptation, studies now tend to highlight the ways in which differences of gender, caste, class, age, ethnicity and so on shape humans' interactions with nature. Diverse groups, even within the same locality, have different values and interests, and conflicting values are struggled over and negotiated in resource-use contexts. This tradition highlights the need to develop a disaggregated understanding of human–environment relationships, and sensitivity to the micropolitics of resource use.

Heterogeneity within communities is particularly evident in terms of gender. Women and men have different roles in activities involving natural resources (including collection and processing). They also have different levels of control over resources. All of this translates into different interests and needs and means that women and men are affected differently by environmental change and conservation or natural resource management activities and policies. Not only do women have different resource needs from men, and different levels of control over resources, but different categories (not necessarily coherent groups) of women differ from each other in these respects. For example, women-headed households are often the poorest and most vulnerable in rural areas. This is obviously relevant to addressing poverty through conservation. Gender perspectives have been a significant development in social science thinking about both the environment and poverty and it is clear that efforts to address poverty and conservation must take account of women's needs and seek new opportunities.

Box 2.3 presents some examples of the interconnections between gender, poverty and conservation. Environmental conditions, natural resource availability and environmental degradation often have specific impacts on women because of their cultural and social activities. Conservation and sustainable development activities may also have specific effects on women, both negative and positive. A clear understanding of the interests of women in relation to natural resource conditions and changes can help to minimize negative impacts and maximize positive impacts.

In an examination of gender policies in Joint Forest Management in India, Locke (1999) argues for the application of a gender and development (GAD) perspective that requires gender analysis as a prerequisite to intervention. Gender analysis is necessary because the power and interests of different groups (including different groups of women) are context specific:

Gender analysis cannot distil any general relationship between women and the environment which could inform prescriptive policy but rather suggests that environmental interventions will be a new arena in which gendered bargaining processes will be enacted and contested. (Locke, 1999, p269)

Box 2.3 Gender, poverty, environment and conservation

Environmental conditions, access to natural resources and environmental degradation have specific impacts on women:

> [Two] billion people around the world have no access to regular energy sources. More than one billion in developing countries have no access to potable water. 2.4 billion people... cannot count on an improved sanitary structure. The lack of potable water, of adequate sanitary conditions and of a regular energy source represent a heavy burden on women who must work to prepare, cook and conserve foods, clean their homes and wash, while at the same time being responsible for the nutrition and health of their families. (Lara, undated a)
>
> For many women the daily task of obtaining safe water for the family is their most pressing problem. As water sources dry up, become choked with silt or contaminated by pollution, the provision of this essential basic resource becomes increasingly difficult. Not only do women have to walk further, and wait longer at the water points, but the return journey, carrying the heavy load, can damage their health. (Rodda, 1991, p84)

A study in Uttaranchal, India, found miscarriages to be five times the national average at 30% and links this to carrying heavy loads of water and fuel during pregnancy. In Nepal, women suffer a high level of uterine prolapse, which is associated with carrying heavy loads of wood soon after childbirth. In contrast, men of the developing world spend about one-tenth of their time that women do on this daily task. (Lara, undated b)

Conservation and sustainable development activities have specific impacts on women (both negative and positive):

Women in the hill areas of Nepal are usually responsible for collecting fuelwood. Closure or protection of degraded forests for regeneration or plantation often adds significantly to workloads as women have to travel further to collect fuel.

In the northern areas of Pakistan, a project promoted on-farm fodder species as an alternative to grazing in high pastures. Because women were responsible for work in the fields, this added to their workload. Women apparently regarded this as acceptable, however, because they saw an overall benefit to their families.

In Shinyanga (Tanzania) the development of *ngitili* (forest enclosures) through community action – supported by a government project and policy – has led to a significant increase in forest tree cover and quality (see Case 2, Chapter 3). This has made it easier for women to collect fuelwood. One woman reported that it used to take five hours to collect fuelwood and that it now takes half an hour. She said that this was especially good because it gave her time to prepare food for her children before they went to school.

Source: Except where otherwise indicated these examples come from the field experience of the authors

In an example that illustrates how apparently reasonable interventions might limit options for women, Locke refers to a team that 'identified poor women's collection of leaves for sale as a "gender need"' (p278). They were criticized by a high-caste woman (who was not one of the leaf collectors), who 'pointed out that this work was a sign of women's desperation, drawing their attention to its arduous, low paid and stigmatized nature' (p278). This is an important theme in poverty reduction: concentration on meeting immediate needs may not address the dimension of powerlessness that is a key element of poverty.

The strength of much of the literature on gender and poverty in conservation is very much in terms of analysis. There is a great deal of literature that shows how women and men use the environment differently and there is a great deal of literature that shows how environmental change affects women differently. There are some very useful tools for gender analysis (see, for example, Espinosa, 2004), but there is relatively little documenting successful interventions or activities that have reduced women's poverty through innovative conservation activities.

Emphasizing diversity in social science thinking is very important when linking poverty reduction and conservation. If different groups of stakeholders have different access to resources and use resources in different ways, then they will be rich or poor in different ways and changes in access to resources will affect them differently. This means that actions and policies need to recognize these different needs, and that actions that are beneficial to one group may be detrimental to another. The impacts of policies need to be examined both within and between groups, not just for broad categories (such as 'all women').

The DFID livelihoods framework

DFID has developed a livelihoods framework (Chambers and Conway, 1992)[9] as a means of assessing the assets that people have to support their livelihoods and it provides a way of thinking about developing and supporting sustainable livelihoods. We do not intend to discuss this framework in detail here but there are two key ideas that are very useful.

The first idea is that there a five types of resources ('capitals') that can support livelihoods. These are:

1. natural capital, such as forests and fisheries;
2. financial capital, such as income opportunities;
3. physical capital, such as infrastructure;
4. human capital, such as knowledge and skills;
5. social capital, such as social networks.

The livelihoods framework thus breaks down capital (or productive assets) into a number of distinct types. In this way of thinking natural resources and the environment can be an asset, as can other capitals.

The second important idea is that it is the way these capitals interact, and especially the transforming structures or processes that are put in place, that turns them into useful elements of a livelihood strategy. A simple example of a transforming structure or process might be a policy change in a case where forest dwelling people were not permitted to harvest and sell timber. A change in laws governing tenure would enable them to turn a potential asset (or capital) into something useful for livelihoods (and poverty reduction). Another example is the development of a marketing structure to enable people to sell shrimp to international markets. Institutional arrangements are often transforming structures or processes.

The crucial advance is the recognition that assets do not always simply turn into livelihoods. Enabling mechanisms are often needed to help them make this transition. This has implications for interventions that attempt to integrate conservation and poverty-focused development. Causal relationships are not simple or unchanging. There are often mechanisms that mediate between causes and effects, and interventions may need to focus on them rather than on apparently direct causes.

Institutions

Institutions can be important 'enabling' mechanisms. The idea of institutions is a useful conceptual tool for understanding how peoples' interactions with each other and the environment are mediated by rules and agreements. This book places great importance on the concept of institutions and how, at various levels (global, national, local), and in various forms (economic or social), they can be modified or crafted to support conservation and poverty reduction (see Box 2.4). Aspects of economic institutions are also discussed in Chapter 5.

Box 2.4 The concept of 'institution'

Institutions can be defined as norms, rules of behaviour and accepted ways of doing things. They can be formal rules (such as laws) or informal (norms). Uphoff (1986) uses the term 'institution' to refer to a set of shared norms and behaviours. (Institutions are not the same as organizations, which Uphoff describes as structures of recognized and accepted roles. Some institutions, such as universities, are also organizations.) The *ngitili* described in the Shinyanga case in Chapter 3 are examples of institutions. The term refers to a particular type of unit of land and implies a shared understanding of rights and behaviour and a set of agreed arrangements for land use.

Institutions relevant to natural resource use and management include rules governing access to resources (tenure), government laws and policies that are intended to determine the way resources are managed, arrangements for decision making about resource use and arrangements for distributing benefits for resource use.

Political ecology

Political ecology is a field of study that looks at the political dimensions of the environment, and is particularly relevant in exploring the ways in which conservation and environmental management are inherently political. Political ecology has generally been interested in how communities, resource management and the environment are being transformed by the global economy through market integration and commercialization (Blaikie and Brookfield, 1987). It has drawn attention to the importance of historical contexts of environmental and social change, and how links between international, regional and national processes interact with local ones. It notes how the political and economic power of different actors and institutions, at various scales, influence social and environmental interactions, and it recognizes the plurality of perceptions of ecological change. Political ecology helps provide a much-needed historical depth to understanding processes of environmental degradation and an appreciation of how power relationships and processes work within particular resource contexts. Political ecology asks who gets what and who controls nature. Conflict over environmental resources is a central concern of a political ecological approach.

Power can be defined in many ways. The key element is the capacity to influence the outcome of events; somebody has power to the extent that she or he can influence outcomes. In the context of natural resource use and conservation:

> *Power can be thought of as the capacity to have a meaningful (effective) input into making and implementing decisions about how forests [and other natural resources] are used and managed. Having a meaningful role does not mean that an actor makes all decisions, but that his/her interests are given serious attention in negotiations.*
>
> *Meaningful decision-making also involves implementation. If a decision cannot be implemented or enforced, then the role in decision-making does not involve effective power. (Fisher, 2003, p20)*

This definition of power fits with the notion of poverty as the deficiency of capabilities. Empowerment is an important aspect of enhancing capabilities and, thus, of contributing to poverty reduction.

An increased interest in how power affects poverty has contributed to a recognition of the need to look at different stakeholders and actors at all levels, from the state to the community. The heterogeneous nature of communities, both in terms of power and wealth, is now recognized as crucial to understanding how resource decisions are made. This has implications for the ways in which greater equity in decision making can be achieved.

Conclusions

This chapter provides some background to attempts to deal with poverty and conservation issues. Some concepts and theories have been identified that can help in understanding possible linkages between poverty reduction and conservation.

Chapter 3 looks at some case studies that provide insights on connections between conservation and poverty and on some of the issues that can inform initiatives for integrating conservation and poverty reduction.

Notes

1   The argument and text in this section draw heavily upon Jeanrenaud (2002).
2   The Conference on the Conservation of Nature and Natural Resources in Modern African States, held in Arusha, Tanganyika (now Tanzania).
3   The very idea of wild Africa, in many ways the iconic wild place, can also be seen as a 'myth' in this sense. Adams and McShane (1992) argue that the whole approach to conservation in Africa has been moulded by the perception of early travellers, writers, hunters and administrators that Africa was essentially a wild paradise, being threatened and destroyed by its native people. Early conservationists felt it was their duty to defend nature from these humans. In fact, Adams and McShane argue, Africa was never wild in this sense and humans have been part of 'nature' throughout human history.
4   One example of nature tourism leading to population increase in areas surrounding a national park is Nepal's Chitwan National Park. An extensive tourist industry, including hotels, lodges, restaurants and tour services, has developed.
5   Personal observation by one of the authors.
6   Many of the criticisms of the assumptions of homogeneity come from social scientists and advocates of more people-friendly approaches to conservation (Agrawal, 1997; Leach et al, 1997). Further, the idea that communities share similar goals to conservationists is frequently challenged by anthropological studies (Ellen, 1986; Croll and Parkin, 1992; Milton, 1993). These and similar problems with the notion of community have spurred developments in differentiating 'user groups' and 'stakeholders' in natural resource management.
7   The idea of 'locally resident' here also includes mobile peoples. Although they are not resident in a relatively small local territory, they are residents in a wider landscape. And although their presence in particular parts of the landscape is seasonal or intermittent, they nevertheless have a close connection with it.
8   Blaikie (2006) argues that CBNRM has largely failed to deliver benefits for communities and, using examples from two countries in Africa, suggests that this is primarily a result of relations between donors and recipient states that take little account of local communities.

9   We refer to the DFID livelihoods framework, although other agencies such as UNDP, Oxfam and CARE have developed and applied similar frameworks. The DFID framework has been widely accepted and is a convenient basis for discussion. For an overview and comparison of the various livelihoods approaches see Carney et al (1999).

3

Case Studies

It is important to ground this discussion in real-world examples. Many of these examples are included in the text itself or in the boxes. Five more detailed cases are included in this chapter. Each of these cases raises a number of points that will be relevant in later chapters. Each case study is intended to be self-contained. Although the case studies are not in a standard format because they were originally prepared for separate purposes, some key points are highlighted in each case.

Although the five cases were each successful in many respects, they are not necessarily presented as models of how to combine conservation with poverty reduction. One of the premises of this book is that such successes have been limited. The cases are presented because they illustrate points relevant to our argument. These are some of the most important points:

- There are many cases where community action, motivated primarily by wellbeing concerns or livelihood needs rather than by conservation as such, has led to improved conservation outcomes. People clearly benefit from the availability of good natural resources.
- Local action may not lead to perfect conservation outcomes, but the results are often better than any realistic alternatives. It is often the failure of government policies and actions that leads to local action in the first place.
- Improved conservation and poverty reduction outcomes often result from institutional changes (policy, development of appropriate local organizations and networks, etc.) at different levels.

Case Study 1
Pred Nai Community Forest, Trad Province, Thailand[1]

Jaruwan Kaewmahanin, Somsak Sukwong and R. J. Fisher

Introduction

Forest management activities were undertaken in a mangrove forest in Thailand by the Pred Nai Community Forestry Group. The village of Pred Nai is located in Trad Province near the Cambodia border. Although the mangrove forest is technically under the authority of the Royal Forest Department (now part of the Ministry of the Environment), this has not prevented community action.[2]

The community in Pred Nai is trying to ensure that the local forest (one of the last remaining mangrove forests on Thailand's eastern seaboard) is managed sustainably. Villagers in Pred Nai have been concerned with the degradation of marine resources, which they consider is mainly due to the destruction of mangrove forests.

In 1985, villagers became concerned when nearby logging concessions over-harvested the mangrove and prohibited villagers from harvesting crabs, shellfish, fish and other resources in the concession areas. Other local interests converted degraded mangrove areas into shrimp farms and built a gate to block seawater, which further damaged the mangrove ecology. In 1986 the villagers formed a group to stop the logging and shrimp farming. Their efforts were successful and the gate was destroyed. Commercial logging was also halted.

Even after the concessions stopped, it was difficult to prevent outsiders, from both nearby villages and farther away, from harvesting or destroying resources within the mangrove area. Local leaders were fearful of any harvesting and did not allow anyone to fish in the mangrove conservation area. This affected the poorest villagers and fishers, whose livelihoods depended on the mangroves.

In response to these events, the villagers began to develop a management plan for the mangrove forest. This involved resource mapping and forest patrols. Pred Nai villagers drew upon the strengths of local traditions and village elders and, with the support of a respected monk, urged people to contribute to a village savings fund that provided a base for their efforts.

As the first management activity, the villagers planted trees in the denuded mangrove area; some stands began to regenerate naturally under strict village protection. Harvesting regulations for the grapsoid crab *(Metopographus sp.)* were developed in 1997. These involved closing the harvest during the breeding period in October. These small crabs are collected mainly for sale. For the other economically important species of mud crab *(Scylla serra)*, villagers set out to increase production by starting a 'crab bank'. People who caught egg-bearing crabs were asked to put them in one of the cages established by the management group in the canals.

The villagers also took action to prevent destructive fishing practices and are experimenting with thinning the dense natural stands of *Ceriops*. The villagers exchange ideas with fishery researchers to help with monitoring methods and collecting relevant data. The process and results are analysed and reflected in the subsequent planning cycle. This conscious learning process is an important aspect of the group's success.

The villagers realized that the people of a single community could not implement successful and sustainable forest management, especially since boundaries were not demarcated and there were no regulations on forest use. A mangrove network developed among a number of other local villages. The idea of networking was initiated and facilitated in those villages that shared boundaries with Pred Nai; it later expanded to many other villages. The communities all became members of the Community Coastal Resource Management Network, Trad Province. Through exchanging information and experiences, the villagers have learned from their successes and failures. Their collaboration has allowed them to initiate new ideas and practices that respond to community needs.[3]

Poverty reduction and improve livelihoods

For some of the villagers the mangrove ecosystem is a valuable source of income; for the village as a whole it is the basis of a way of life. The village is not particularly poor, but crab collecting is mainly carried out by relatively poor members of the community.[4] (Not all poor villagers are involved and those involved are not necessarily the poorest.) For the people involved, crab collecting is very important for income and livelihood security. The management initiative has helped to ensure that the environmentally and economically important mangrove area is managed sustainably. Local management efforts have also spurred other community development activities.

According to information provided by villagers, the income level of some villagers involved in crab collecting has almost doubled as a result of improved catches of grapsoid crab. Other statements suggest that the level of income from crab collection has remained about the same. While exact figures on income are not available, data suggest that the poorer villagers engaged in crab collection could earn 600–700 THB (US$15–18) per day. It is clear that collectors can now collect the crabs much more quickly as a result of greater availability, particularly in the low season; this provides opportunities for additional economic activity. In this way the increased availability of crabs has enhanced livelihood security.

According to information obtained in 2004, the average daily harvest of grapsoid crab has increased since 1998 from 8 to 15 kilograms per collector per day. The Pred Nai community is now developing a marketing system, processing crackers made from mangrove plants and producing local wine.

Increased mud crab harvests, resulting from the innovative introduction of crab banks, have also been reported. Artificial fish 'houses' (made from blocks of used car tyres) are now being installed in canals. According to villagers and outsiders, this means that less time is needed for fish harvesting. Pred Nai villagers are now trying to restore the seacoast within a 3000-metre conservation zone and protect it from destructive fishing practices such as the use of push nets and trawlers.

The community forestry project has also encouraged the villagers to initiate other economic activities. A savings management group, formed in 1995, had more than 600 members and a fund totalling nearly 6 million THB (about US$72,000) in 2004. Other community organizations were established, such as a women's group, a youth group and a network of people from various villages who use the mangrove area. The management initiative has also encouraged other villages to set up community forests.

Effect on biodiversity

The project began with restoration of the mangrove forest through plantation and protection, which led to the regeneration of mangrove trees. After 16 years of community action faunal biodiversity has increased; villagers report that stocks of crab, shellfish and fish have also grown. Many water birds like the painted stork *(Mycteria leucocephala), Parphyris poliocephalus,* purple heron *(Ardea purpurea),* grey heron *(A. cineria), Dendrocygna javanica* and Brahminy kite *(Haliastur indus)* are returning and macaques *(Macaca fascicularis)* have been reported as coming back after moving away during the logging period. 'Hoy lod' or razor clams *(Solen strictus Gould.)*, absent for 20 years, have also reappeared.

After a couple of years of protection and some conflicts over the use of forest resources, villagers are now trying more proactive methods of management; they are emphasizing sustained use rather than more passive conservation. One of the most valuable local species is the mud crab. It is especially prized because of its rarity due to the fact that so few mangroves remain. Some villagers who were interested in cultivating the mud crab formed a group in order to increase production. They exchange ideas among themselves and are in contact with fishery researchers who specialize in crab aquarium breeding.

There is a debate in conservation literature about whether sustained use and conservation of biodiversity are compatible (see, for example, Robinson, 1999). In the case of Pred Nai, and no doubt in many other cases of community-based conservation, previous use had severely affected biodiversity. This community-based initiative has led to both increased income and improved biodiversity. The community activity did not so much 'conserve' biodiversity as reintroduce it.

Additional impacts

Education is another important factor. Villagers have collaborated with the schools and village elders to teach school children about mangrove ecology and coastal resources, using the mangrove community forest as a learning laboratory. Boys and girls join adult villagers in the planting programme and the forest-thinning experiment. The villagers have also constructed a walkway in the mangrove for educational purposes.

The Asia-Pacific Economic Community (APEC) sponsored a group of school children from various countries to attend an environmental camp and carry out fieldwork at Pred Nai in July 2003. The students learned about mangrove and coastal resources, leading to a real sense of pride in the community.

The self-taught approach is a major factor in the success of Pred Nai. Villagers started with reflection and then developed their abilities to solve problems, learning new ways to manage the resources, their village and their own lives.

Partnerships

The success of the initiative depended not just on managing the mangrove area but on managing the people who use the mangrove. Management activities incorporated innovative partnerships and a wide range of participants.

After the mangrove concessions ended and a management group was set-up, local users who depended on the area were not allowed to harvest any products. This caused resentment and conflicts. After discussions with community members, however, the villagers slowly began experimenting with less restrictive management and the committee became more inclusive.

Partnerships needed to be established with people from other villages who wished to use the resources. Villagers set up a People's Mangrove Forest Network, which meets in different villages on a rotating basis.

Villagers have gained experience in working collaboratively with outsiders such as fishery experts, foresters and other institutions. Since some problems are beyond the scope of village action, these relationships with other institutions are important. They include networks with other villages, collaboration with other institutions, such as government forestry and fishery departments, police patrols and politicians. Religious institutions, such as temples in the Eastern Gulf region, have also been important partners.

The other main participants are the local officials. Although local management efforts are not legally recognized by the national government, local officials have provided technical and moral support. The provincial governor became an active supporter of the community forest and the mangrove network after he saw what local efforts had achieved. An important lesson is that legal recognition is not always essential if there is a collective interest and vision in managing resources.

Sustainability

The initiative operated at the local level and increased the learning capacity of community members. They also learned to communicate and collaborate with outsiders. In the early days of community action, villagers contacted the ministerial level of government for help; when problems arose within the community or in the vicinity, they initiated local solutions. The villagers' success has become so well known that many study tours from abroad have come to visit them. Ecotourism is also being discussed. Both of these outcomes have potential benefits and risks.

Pred Nai is a good example of innovation in natural resource management and in using income savings for village development. Not just the forest but the broader landscape (including orchards, canals and the sea) is being managed, conserved and sustained.

Local efforts will be sustained as long as there are economic, environmental and cultural interests in managing the mangrove area. A potential threat to the initiative is restrictive and intrusive national legislation that usurps the rights and efforts of the local villagers in the name of the national interest.

Political and legislative context

In 2002, Pred Nai Community Forest was awarded a prize by the Royal Forest Department. This is ironic given the fact that legislative support for local management efforts has been debated for more than a decade in Thailand. On the surface, the ingredients for cooperative management are all there: communities throughout Thailand are managing and protecting forests, and the Constitution stipulates that local communities have the right to participate in natural resource management. On closer inspection, however, many obstacles still exist.

The policy reform process has stagnated and conflicts are becoming more acute. Local networks of community forestry groups are pitted against a powerful coalition of bureaucrats, academics and environmentalists who perceive rural people as destructive and their participation as a threat to national interests.

Since 1992, following pressure from people's organizations and their supporters there have been a number of versions of a Community Forestry Bill. Alternate versions of the Bill have taken liberal or restrictive positions in terms of community rights. In early March 2000, a 'people's version' was submitted to the Thai parliament after 52,698 signatures were collected for a petition. A parliamentary commission was set up to examine the bill and previous community forestry bills but was cancelled after only three months when parliament was dissolved.

In response, a mass media campaign was initiated to lobby for changes to parliamentary regulations and more inclusive parliamentary commissions. After a new government was elected, a new commission was set up. One third of its members were peoples' representatives. The commission finalized the draft bill, which was then approved by the lower house of parliament.

Unfortunately, the bill's intent and focus was drastically changed by the senate upper house. The crucial part of that version of the bill, Article 18, stated that those people settled in national parks, wildlife sanctuaries and watersheds prior to the date the forests were declared protected could continue to manage and make sustainable use of forest products. The senate deleted this provision. There were various reasons for this. Some senators said they were afraid that if the villagers received rights to manage the forest, they would convert the fertile forest to grow cash crops; others felt that 'outsiders' might abuse the bill by encroaching on protected forest and then claiming the right to manage it.

Another version of the bill was finally passed in late 2007, but as of April 2008 it had not received Royal Assent and objections had been lodged with the High Court on constitutional grounds. This act is more restrictive than desired by some supporters of community forestry.

Conclusion

Community-based initiatives in general, and Pred Nai in particular, should not be romanticized. There have been differences of opinion and conflict within Pred Nai about mangrove management, including debate about preservation versus sustainable use. What is important is that the community members have managed this conflict themselves, through negotiation and dialogue.

Pred Nai shows that communities can work cooperatively and that community initiatives can lead to improved biodiversity. Although biodiversity had been compromised, largely as the result of outside commercial interests and government policies, it has improved immensely since villagers have regained control. Pred Nai is an example of people empowering themselves through local initiative and organization, demonstrating that confidence can be gained through small successes and that it can help improve livelihoods and contribute to reduced poverty.

Notes

1   This is a revised and updated version of a paper originally prepared for distribution at the workshop session on Community Conserved Areas at the World Parks Congress, 8–17 August 2003, Durban. Although the paper has been updated with regard to recent policy changes, it reports on research carried out prior to 2005. The paper is based on experiences gained in an action research project carried out in Pred Nai by RECOFTC in collaboration with the community and funded by the Toyota Foundation. We wish to thank the people of Pred Nai for their cooperation and enthusiasm and Supaporn Worrapornphan for her continuing contribution to supporting the efforts of the Pred Nai community and for providing additional data in 2004. Somjai Srimongkontip and Michael Nurse also provided additional information based on fieldwork carried out in November 2004. We also wish to thank Jim Enright for help in providing the scientific names of marine species and for advice on mangrove ecology.

2   The Fisheries Department has no legal authority but assists with the management of mangrove aquatic animals.

3   A video in Thai and English, 'A Community Coastal Resource Management Network in Trad Province' (RECOFTC, 2002) has been produced about this networking activity. Pred Nai also appears in the film 'Forests, Local Knowledge and Livelihoods' (IFAD/RECOFTC, 2000).
4   Some students and other more wealthy members of the community collect crabs on a fairly casual basis for consumption.

Lessons for this book

- Community-initiated conservation at Pred Nai helped improve livelihoods and increase incomes of the people involved in crab collection – generally the poorer members of the community. This is an excellent example of the potential for locally initiated natural resource restoration in poverty reduction.
- In terms of the World Bank's three dimensions of poverty and the DFID livelihoods framework, the community action addressed poverty through building assets for the poor (improving natural capital) and empowering people to take greater control over their own resources. This was achieved through building and applying social capital (the capacity to work cooperatively) and increasing skills and confidence (human capital).
- Community action can sometimes protect resources where government agencies cannot. It may be able to alleviate problems caused by government agencies and policies (as with the charcoal logging concessions and shrimp farm promotion).
- The biodiversity outcome of community action, though not perfect, was far better than it would have been had previous state policies and practices continued.
- Adaptive community learning is important.
- Legal recognition is not essential if there is community interest and vision. Nevertheless, the lack of supporting legislation and policy is potentially a major constraint to the sustainability of the community actions.

Case Study 2
Forest restoration in Shinyanga, Tanzania[1]

E. Barrow and W. Mlenge

Introduction

Shinyanga region, in northwest Tanzania, is divided into six districts and 833 villages. The predominantly semi-arid region has nearly two million people. The high population density of 42 people per square kilometre, combined with an expansive agropastoral land-use system and subsistence and cash cropping have exacerbated an already serious problem of land clearing for cultivation. Clearing started in the colonial era to eradicate the tsetse fly and has been perpetuated to increase the area under cultivation, especially for cotton and rice. The Sukuma people are agropastoralists; their major crops include maize, sorghum, millet, cassava, cotton and rice. Over 80 per cent of the population owns and manages livestock on communal rangelands (Hendy, 1980). Higher livestock densities and the expansion of cash crop cultivation have resulted in acute fodder shortages, especially during the long dry seasons (Otsyina et al, 1993).

Detailed local knowledge exists about the values and uses of different tree species. Of particular importance is the Sukuma practice of *ngitili* grazing and fodder reserves. This practice is known throughout the region and is culturally well established (Barrow et al, 1992). In Shinyanga the practice of *ngitili* or 'enclosure' conserves rangelands for use in the dry seasons by maintaining an area of standing hay until the next rains (Barrow et al, 1992). *Ngitili* are divided into sections; each section is completely grazed before the next is opened.

The practice developed in response to acute fodder shortages due to drought, diminishing grazing land due to increased cropping, rapidly declining land productivity, and shortages of herding labour (Otsyina et al, 1993; Kilahama, 1994; Maro, 1997). There are two types of *ngitili*: family or individual reserves, and communal reserves. Family reserves are established on an individual's land in fallow; communal reserves can be made on any land suitable for dry-season grazing. Communal *ngitili* are found along riverbeds and hill areas.

Previously the Shinyanga region was extensively forested (Malcolm, 1953), varying from *Miombo* woodland to acacia bushland in the drier areas, but several factors have contributed to forest and woodland degradation (Barrow et al, 1988):

- Cash crop expansion – in the early 1900s agricultural production in Shinyanga region was subsistence based; sorghum and millet were the main crops. By the early 1940s, large-scale cultivation of cotton and tobacco was introduced, accompanied by extensive clearing of forests (Kaale and Gillusson, 1985; Maro, 1997).

- Declining soil fertility – over 90 per cent of the people depend on agriculture but the extent of arable land is decreasing due to soil erosion and loss of soil fertility, combined with poor agriculture and livestock practices. This exacerbates the existing degradation of land and natural resources (Kerario and Nanai, 1995).
- Livestock – livestock are a vital part of Sukuma economy and provide insurance against periods of hardship. The remaining grazing land is generally overstocked, since much of the available land has been converted for cultivation (Barrow et al, 1992). This results in reduced grass and herb cover, an increased dominance of unpalatable species, a further loss of important browse species (which can no longer regenerate easily), and an overall loss of soil quality (Kerario and Nanai, 1995; Vice President's Office, 1997).
- Villagization – under traditional systems, the ownership and management of land tenure rights over *ngitili* and land in Shinyanga were governed by local bylaws. After independence, the Villages and Ujamaa Villages Act (1975) was introduced that relocated farmers from traditional villages to newly created settlements. Household assets – including houses, farms and *ngitili* – were often abandoned (Otsyina et al, 1993). This upheaval was exacerbated by increases in numbers of both people and livestock. The new village pattern, although administratively advantageous, made traditional adaptation to local ecological conditions more difficult. It has led, for example, to the breakdown of some traditional soil conservation practices (Barrow et al, 1988).
- Wood demand – the demand for fuelwood, which increased along with the population, has exceeded supply, resulting in accelerated rates of deforestation. People must travel long distances (more than 10 kilometres) to fetch wood. Many women in Shinyanga increasingly use twigs, stalks and animal manure instead of wood (Ministry of Community Development, 1996).

Legislative and policy framework

In order to address these problems, the government implemented a conservation and restoration project in Shinyanga region called Hifadhi ardhi Shinyanga (Soil Conservation Shinyanga or HASHI). The Sukuma people suggested that restoring *ngitili* was the best way to meet local needs. The restoration effort was based on the following factors:

- the local need for woodland restoration to supply goods and services;
- a desire by the people to invest in restoration;
- pre-existing management institutions;
- the ability of HASHI to provide extension, training and technical advice.

In 1998 Tanzania approved its revised forest policy, which places a strong emphasis on participatory management and decentralization. The principles of multiple-use forests, where biodiversity conservation and management guidelines are incorporated in management plans, have been adopted. Local communities are encouraged to participate in the management of forests through collaborative and community-based forest management. Villagers and communities select and set aside degraded and village forested areas to be conserved and managed as village forests (Barrow et al, 2002).

Village boundaries have been surveyed to help villages obtain village title deeds and individuals obtain title deeds within village land. This helps secure village and farm lands, and is an incentive for future improvement. The National Land Policy of 1997, the Land Act of 1999 and the Village Act of 1999 have actively supported the formal establishment of *ngitili*. Village governments are increasingly empowered to enact village bylaws to protect their *ngitili*, using traditional rules and village guards.

Poverty reduction

As a result of the HASHI programme, the number and size of *ngitili* increased dramatically. The use of both traditional and scientific knowledge facilitates the restoration of forests and improves community livelihoods (Barrow et al, 1988; Kaale et al, 2002).

During a detailed survey in the late 1990s, it was found that in a sample of 172 villages, there were 18,607 *ngitili* covering an area of about 78,000 hectares (Maro, 1995). The average size of a group or village *ngitili* is 164 hectares, while the average size of an individual *ngitili* was 2.3 hectares. Ninety per cent of the people in the 833 villages of Shinyanga have their own *ngitili*. Based on this, by the year 2000, between 300,000 and 500,000 hectares of *ngitili* had been restored in the 833 villages of the region. The HASHI experience went beyond the dreams of many of the early proponents of the project. *Ngitili* are found throughout all villages and districts, and almost all respondents (90 per cent) have access to them.

Ngitili are becoming a key component of Sukuma land-use management and meet many of the needs of the local people:

- they provide a source of dry-season forage for livestock;
- they ensure that people can obtain fuel and poles without having to walk long distances;
- they allow people access to medicinal plants, which is particularly important as 'formal' health services become increasingly expensive;
- they provide a place where people can harvest wild fruits and foods, even during a drought;
- they lessen the risks of dry periods and drought, thereby enhancing the resilience of the overall system;
- they are a source of shade and quiet.

Views on *ngitili* improvement and management varied, although they were mostly supportive. About 80 per cent of people admitted that there had been positive changes since the advent of villagization (Maro, 1995). Most farmers (90 per cent) felt that *ngitili* provided several important goods and services: pasture for animals at the most critical time of the year, thatch control of soil erosion, restoration of soil fertility, wood products and income (Maro, 1995).

A review of the social, economic and environmental impacts of forest landscape restoration in Shinyanga (Monela et al, 2004) indicated that *ngitili* have considerable economic and biodiversity values, which have been largely achieved through the restoration of forests. Some of the economic values identified are:

- *Ngitili* are a significant income source, providing an average of US$14 per month per person (approximately US$1000 per family per year) across over 830 villages and approximately 2.25 million people of Shinyanga region.
- Over 64 per cent of households receive significant benefits from *ngitili*.
- Some costs arise from restoration. They are related to the loss of crops (rice, maize, cassava, etc.) due to birds, porcupines, rats, antelope and monkeys. Livestock loss has also occurred; jackals and hyenas hunt goats and sheep. The average annual cost due to problem animals is about US$63 per household per year.

Biodiversity impacts

Although increasing biodiversity was not the objective of the project in Shinyanga, restoring the goods and services provided by woodlands through the regeneration and planting of indigenous trees also helped to restore biodiversity – in terms of tree species as well as grasses and other herbs. It is also very likely that some small fauna have returned to the area.

Some of the biodiversity values reported by Monela et al (2004) are:

- 152 different species of tree, shrub and climber – mainly young trees (restored as a result of closure);
- more than 60 tree species used for various reasons (19 product types in total), medicines, fruits and vegetables, fuelwood, timber and woodcraft, fodder, fencing, bush meat, thatch and shelter;
- 145 bird species, many new to the area as a result of *ngitili*, including seven species with restricted ranges found in Shinyanga;
- 13 grass genus, 25 other herb genus and a number of small mammals, reptiles, etc.

Other impacts

Traditional rules for protecting individual and communal *ngitili* involve guards known as *sungusungu* and community assemblies known as *dagashida*. The fact that most Sukuma people adhere to these traditional arrangements has contributed to the successful management and restoration of *ngitili* (Barrow et al, 1992; Kilahama, 1994; Maro, 1995).

Private *ngitili* can increase a farmer's land value. They are increasing in number, which may reflect a shift from common property to private ownership. Communal *ngitili* help restore degraded areas on hills and river edges. They provide badly needed dry-season forage, reduce soil erosion and conserve catchment areas. They also help lessen the need for agropastoralists to move long distances to seek grazing during the dry season; this reduces livestock theft and disease.

The *ngitili* practice in Shinyanga is also seen as providing multiple natural resources, with an increasing focus on trees. In Shinyanga, decentralization, increased tenure security and the empowering approach of HASHI – combined with the traditional knowledge base about *ngitili* management – provided the impetus for restoration. This demonstrates how traditional institutions, rules and regulations can complement government legislation and policy. The focus of the project shifted from tree planting and soil conservation to catalysing and facilitating a people-driven process.

The institutional responsibilities for the management of *ngitili* are as important as the technical aspects. A community may have a wide range of institutions, such as *sungusungu,* that are concerned with issues such as access, control and responsibilities. To an outsider they may not be obvious; even if they are known, their importance may be underrated in natural resource management (Barrow, 1996). In the case of Shinyanga, these institutions were the foundation of *ngitili* restoration, and HASHI made determined attempts to give control to the village itself (Shepherd et al, 1991). Traditional sanction mechanisms and fines (*mchenya*) have been the basis for enforcement. In dealing with land-use matters, this use of traditional mechanisms – which often operate in near isolation from formal government – is an important feature (Shepherd et al, 1991). Blending traditional and formal institutions has been an important part of the success of *ngitili* restoration. The forestry sector at the local and national level, along with HASHI, has assisted with *ngitili* improvement through boundary and enrichment planting and pasture improvement.

Devolution of control and responsibility to the village level has also been an important factor of the success of *ngitili*. There is an increasing recognition, both in policy and practice, of the importance of the official village government and traditional institutions in the management of *ngitili*.

Sustainability

The Sukuma are shrewd and intelligent managers of a fragile landscape. They have the techniques to foster and enhance tree restoration, and the social structures and institutions to implement it. The case study demonstrates a number of practical lessons for forest and woodland restoration:

- Building on existing knowledge systems is the basis for restoration. A detailed knowledge base existed about the importance of individual species, as did traditional management systems.
- Restoration efforts were integrated into existing rules, regulations and sanctions, which were well understood by the local people.
- A reasonable degree of social coherence and a strong social structure is desirable when implementing improvements and changes.
- External change agents (HASHI, in this case) should support and guide the process rather than dominate or drive it.
- The specific details of a restoration project should not be imposed on participants by outsiders.
- Keeping livestock is consistent with tree and woodland restoration; pastoralists depend on trees for their livestock to browse and forage, and to meet other household and contingency needs.

A combination of these and other factors has allowed for changes in ecological and social attitudes to the restoration of wood and grasslands over a relatively short period of time. These important factors are as follows:

- Restoration processes must be based on common sense, and must be easily replicable.
- A tradition of woodland and tree conservation provided the basis for restoration.
- Increasing local people's ownership of and control over resources, and their capacity to manage them, is essential.
- National and district forests, as well as the smallest areas, are candidates for restoration.
- Because even the smallest areas can be conserved, the practice is more widely applicable. Both 'poor' and 'richer' farmers benefit.
- Generating local interest in natural resource management, for example through enrichment planting, is important.
- A supportive framework of policy and legislation relating to forestry, land tenure and local government reform is essential.
- Real participation and community ownership is imperative.

Some risks

A recent study by PROFOR of Busongo village in Shinyanga (reported by Shepherd, 2008) provides an update on the spread of *ngitili* and identifies some possible risks. The issues raised highlight the importance of developing appropriate institutional arrangements (checks and balances) to avoid the real risks of elite capture and distorted distribution of benefits. Two key issues identified were:

- Claims by poorer women of elite capture by wealthy men who acquired land for private *ngitili* to be used as grazing land at the expenses of too little land being set aside for the communal *ngitil*, useful for poorer users (Shepherd, 2008).
- According to Shepherd (personal communication), the wealthier Busongo residents received greater benefits than the poor. Roughly speaking, forests make an overall contribution of about US$192 per annum (US$16 a month) to the incomes of rich and middling Busongo residents bringing their annual income up to $802, or well above $2 a day. For the poor and very poor, the proportional benefit of forest is higher, but the actual amount is lower. Forests contribute about $50 a year (a little over $4 a month) to per capita income, bringing the total up to $173, which is still less than half the dollar-a-day figure often quoted for the very poor.

If appropriate (internal and external) checks and balances are not in place, then the process can be usurped by the rich and more powerful. Balance and equity need to achieved and constantly renegotiated so that the poorer and less powerful can also improve their livelihood base. Putting in place participatory monitoring (so that all different groups in the village are involved and to ensure that some of those danger signs are picked up and addressed) and evaluation (so that external perspectives can be brought to bear and help point out potential problem areas together with the means to address them) is vital.

This implies that the institutions (village government, traditional groups) that mediate the practice and use of *ngitili* need to be robust, strong, adaptive and resilient enough to cater for changing situations and resolve in a fair and equitable manner evolving problems – such as increased landlessness.

Under Tanzanian Socialism (*Ujamaa*), local government possessed redistributive power under communal land law, especially in cases of inequity and where land was not seen to be productively used, as may often be the case with absentee landlords. As a result tenure rights might be lost. While villages may have buffer areas in the communal village lands (and communal *ngitili*), this is not a long-term solution to issues such as landlessness.

This demonstrates the importance of the need for continued interaction with such a process, ensuring that there are mechanisms to secure equity both within families (gender) and within villages (to reduce elite capture). Here fair and negotiated tenure rights would appear to be essential.

Conclusion

The number and area of *ngitili* restored since 1986 demonstrates the resurgence of a traditional natural resource management system. HASHI was in the right place at the right time, and with the right approach and attitude to help bring about the reality of a restored, locally owned landscape.

Forest and woodland restoration is not just the responsibility of governments. Rural people can and will restore very significant areas with the right incentives and with policies that suit local conditions. In this case the need for dry-season forage for livestock, combined with the increasing need for timber and non-wood forest products, were the two main forces driving the restoration. The areas restored vary in size from individual woodlands on individual farms to large community-based forests. The restored trees and woodlands provide important livelihood benefits, including forage and browse for livestock, foods and fruits for people, medicines and timber products. This has helped people improve their livelihoods and enhanced the resilience of land-use systems, especially in dry periods and droughts.

Note

1   This case study has been modified, abridged and updated from Barrow and Mlenge (2003).

Lessons for this book

- Community action (as in the case of Pred Nai) can lead to significantly improved ecosystems. Even though the goal of the project was not ecosystem restoration, the area affected by forest restoration was very large.
- The success of forest restoration (the conservation outcome) was a result of local people restoring forest ecosystem function as a livelihood resource. This was not motivated by a concern with conservation as such, but the conservation results were positive.
- Government policy (the villagization programme), which advocated removal of trees, contributed significantly to the original environmental degradation. This is an example of the way in which even well-intentioned policies can have serious negative results.
- Local environmental knowledge was an important factor in the success of the restoration. The reinvigoration of traditional institutional arrangements (*ngitili*, *dagashida* and *sungusungu*) was an essential ingredient.
- There is no simple causal relationship between population growth and environmental degradation. Conservation improved in Shinyanga at the same time that the population was increasing. Institutional arrangements (at the local level to restore and empower traditional institutions and at the policy level to remove policies that encouraged forest degradation and replace them with supportive policies) transformed pressures to degrade the environment into incentives to restore it.
- One of the major contributions of the HASHI programme was allowing traditional institutions to function. This worked by removing constraints.
- Access to control over resources increases the willingness of individuals and

groups to manage them sustainably. The development of an enabling policy framework contributed to this.

- Although it is often assumed that the main opportunities for combining conservation and livelihoods come from high-value resources, restoration of degraded environments can have major conservation and livelihood benefits.
- The outcomes of the project were largely a result of building social capital (appropriate local institutions which enhanced cooperation), restoring natural capital and developing transforming structures.
- The case study highlights some of the risks of elite capture and inequitable distribution of benefits that are often present in small projects and large programmes alike. Implications are the need for careful monitoring of unintended consequences, the importance of checks and balances, and the need for a self-critical approach on the part of intervening agencies.

Case Study 3
The NAFRI-IUCN NTFP Project in Lao PDR[1]

Jason Morris, Andrew Ingles and Sounthone Ketpanh

The National Agriculture and Forestry Research Institute (NAFRI) and the International Union for Conservation of Nature (IUCN), with funding from the Royal Netherlands Embassy, jointly executed a non-timber forest project in Lao PDR from July 1995 to September 2001. The project was designed as an ICDP. Its goal was to conserve forest biodiversity by promoting the sustainable economic exploitation of NTFPs at the community and provincial level (Ingles and Karki, 2001). Following a reformulation of objectives during a mid-term review in 1998, the project sought to achieve this goal by doing the following (summarized from Donovan et al, 1998):

- demonstrating sustainable systems of NTFP use that contribute to forest and biodiversity conservation;
- developing a strategy, in cooperation with government agencies and other relevant organizations, to expand the application of these systems;
- laying the groundwork for a national management strategy for NTFPs.

As an ICDP, the project had a vested interest in supporting livelihoods and community development. One of the five components of the sustainable NTFP systems was wellbeing which involved reducing pressure on forests and improving the ability and motivation of village communities to manage forests by improving their wellbeing through increasing income and improving basic village infrastructure (Donovan et al, 1998). Although this approach was initially described as 'conservation through economic incentives' (Ingles and Hicks, 2002), it was found during project implementation that the links between livelihoods and conservation were much more extensive than had been realized. The reconceptualized approach can be called 'conservation by removing constraints' (Ingles and Hicks, 2002). Addressing poverty issues promoted conservation in the following ways:

- by removing some of the poverty-related factors that drive over-exploitation of NTFPs by local people;
- by empowering local people to better control the access and use of forests by outsiders;
- by organizing local people to better coordinate their own behaviour through institution building.

The NTFP project in Oudomxay province provides an example of how poverty reduction and environment conservation can be mutually reinforcing objectives.

Nam Pheng village in Oudomxay province

Oudomxay province is located in northwest Lao PDR and shares part of its border with China. Nam Pheng village is a two-hour drive north of the provincial capital and 21 kilometres from the capital of Na Mo District. China is less than half an hour away.

Nam Pheng village was established in 1973. The people in Nam Pheng are Lao Theung from the Khamou Ou, Leua and Rok ethnic groups. They speak the Khamou language and are mainly upland cultivators, using shifting cultivation. The village is organized with a village committee, comprising the village chief and deputy, the chief of security and representatives from village unions for youth, women, elders, agriculture, forestry, education and health.

When the NTFP project began in 1996, the village contained 43 households with 244 people. People cultivated an average of one hectare per household per year; each hectare yielded approximately 1.2 tonnes. They maintained fallow cycles of seven to nine years. Most households also raised livestock, primarily cows but also pigs and buffalo. The nearest school was in the neighbouring village of Na Hom, but attendance was reported to be low. Water for drinking and residential use came mostly from a stream passing through the village. Illnesses, especially diarrhoea and malaria, were prevalent. The villagers' main source of cash income was NTFPs, which were generally collected and bartered on a small scale. Bamboo shoots were sold to traders who exported them to China and Thailand.

Project activities

The NTFP project supported a number of initiatives in Nam Pheng: a village rice bank; a water supply system; construction of a school; domestication trials for *Sa Pan* (paper mulberry), cardamom and eaglewood; forest land allocation; and the establishment of marketing groups and sustainable harvesting regimes for bitter bamboo shoots and wild cardamom (Ingles and Karki, 2001).

One of the most important initiatives supported by the NTFP project was the rice bank. This addressed the villagers' most pressing need: food security. Although the rice bank related only indirectly to NTFP conservation it built trust in the conservation project, freed up villagers' time for conservation activities, and reduced the threat of overharvesting in the forest. The project subsequently addressed forestland allocation, domestication trials and NTFP marketing.

Forests are allocated communally to each village committee according to traditional village boundaries and mutually agreed borders. Forests in the Nam Pheng area were allocated during 1997 and 1998 in collaboration with the District Agriculture and Forestry Office (DAFO) in Namo. Forestland allocation was an important first step to sustainable harvesting; it gave the village committee authority to resolve resource-use conflicts within the village and to respond to threats from outside. Village forests in Nam Pheng covered a total area of 648 hectares, or 46.5 hectares per household in 1998, including 515 hectares of bitter bamboo forest.

The project helped organize an NTFP marketing group for bitter bamboo. This involved a series of meetings where villagers and project staff gathered information, analysed problems, decided on a management structure, elected members for management, agreed on regulations, planned, trained and implemented the initiative. Anyone who collected bitter bamboo shoots for sale – virtually everyone in Nam Pheng – was allowed to join the group. The management structure consisted of a group committee (which is the village committee) and one-person units for monitoring, accounting and trade. Decisions were made collectively in meetings chaired by the group committee.

An important innovation of the marketing group was training villagers in the use of weighing scales. Previously, villagers simply bartered their NTFPs in bunches to passing traders for clothes, condiments, candies and other items. The use of scales allowed villagers to command higher prices and gave them more confidence when negotiating with traders. The initial results were impressive: sales of bitter bamboo rose to about 54 million kip (approximately US$5400) in 2000, a two–threefold increase. (This represents an average of 40 per cent of household incomes.) Following this success, the marketing group organized a similar regime for cardamom. The marketing group was able to raise the local price for cardamom from 500 kip per kilogram (US$0.05) to 35,000 kip per kilogram (US$3.5) in 1998. Although prices have since dropped to around 12,000–14,000 kip, they are much higher than before the marketing group began its work.

The marketing group sets the dates of the harvesting season each year, based on the natural characteristics and regenerative capacity of each NTFP. (The NTFP project assisted villagers with ecological information and training.) The harvesting season for bitter bamboo usually lasts about four and a half months between December and April, although collection for consumption is permitted throughout the year. The harvesting season for cardamom is much shorter, usually ten days in late August.

Because bamboo shoots command the highest prices when fresh, households sell their stock directly to the group committee at the end of every collection day. The committee then sells on a larger scale to traders. In the case of cardamom, villagers peel and dry it and then sell to the marketing group, usually at the end of harvesting season.

Generally, the individual collector takes 85–90 per cent of the final sale; the remaining 10–15 per cent is put in an NTFP fund. Between 1998 and 2000, 17 million kip (US$1700) had accumulated in the NTFP fund from the sale of bitter bamboo and cardamom. The fund supports community projects (such as the purchase of an electric generator), community services (for example loans) and pays the salaries of the monitoring, accounting and trade units. In 1999 the fund was used to improve the village's water supply system; in 2000 it supported the construction of a school, with financial assistance from the NTFP project, and provided loans to 15 households. Use of the fund and salary levels are decided collectively by the marketing group.

Long-term impacts

The project finished operations in 2001. In 2002 a participatory wealth-ranking exercise was carried out in Nam Pheng (Ingles and Hicks, 2004). All households in the village were ranked into three wealth categories according to wealth criteria developed by a group of villagers:

- Well-off: permanent house, equipment and accessories (e.g. truck, TV/VCD), enough money or rice for one year, some livestock and enough labour.
- Middle: semi-permanent house (i.e. thatched grass roof, stripped bamboo walls), insufficient money or rice for half year, few livestock and enough labour.
- Poor: temporary house (i.e. bamboo or small trees for beams and pillars), insufficient rice for full year, no livestock and insufficient labour. (Ingles and Hicks, 2004, p80)

At the same time a retrospective wealth ranking was carried out based on recall of rankings in 1996, when project activities started in the village. These rankings showed that as far as the 'client' population was concerned there had been a considerable movement of households upwards in wealth categories. Between 1996 and 2002 the numbers of households in well-off and middle categories had each increased by 8 per cent, while the number in the poor category had decreased by 15 per cent. If households formed after 1996 are excluded, the percentage of well-off and middle households increased by 12 per cent and 10 per cent respectively and the number of poor families decreased by 23 per cent.

Several other participatory investigations carried out at the same time as the wealth-ranking exercise (ranking income and expenditure and group discussions of 'changes in livelihoods, forests, and an assessment of gains and losses') demonstrated that the NTFPs targeted by the project (bitter bamboo and cardamom) had become major sources of income and were regarded as a major factor in improvement. In discussions with a number of randomly selected households:

villagers suggested that availability of labour was the main factor for their graduation from poor to middle class. Many of the households were described as having young children and/or an ill family member in 1996. When the children had grown up and ill people had become healthy, the increased labour helped improve household productive capacity... However, participants also acknowledged that increased awareness of markets for NTFPs and, in particular, bitter bamboo was very important. As one member said, 'bitter bamboo shoots solved many problems in our lives. Without bitter bamboo we would be much poorer than we are today'. If increased labour availability was the main factor for overcoming poverty, then collection of NTFPs was the main employer of that labour. (Ingles and Hicks, 2004, p82)

A further wealth-ranking exercise carried out in 2006, five years after the project had ended, suggested that the improved rankings had been maintained and that there had even been a continued improvement since the project ended (Ingles et al, 2006). Fourteen households graduated one wealth class between 1996 and 2002. In this period 'another seven households graduated one wealth class while previous gains were held by all but one household that slipped back a class. Overall, the proportion of households in the poorest wealth class fell from 33% in 1996 to 13% in 2006' (Ingles et al, 2006, p16).

So what were the causes of the improved livelihoods and reduction in poverty at Nam Pheng? One particularly important reason for thinking that project interventions were important in the improved wealth rankings is that the people involved in the ranking themselves attributed the improvement to project interventions.

Ingles et al (2006, p19) suggest the main reasons for poverty reduction in Ban Nampheng were:

1 Food security was achieved, mainly through the NTFP Project's rice bank, forest land-allocation and marketing group interventions that increased the income from NTFP sales from which to buy rice.
2 Available labour increased through improvements in health-care and nutrition.
3 The returns on labour from NTFP collection and sale were increased significantly.
4 Additional labour was applied productively to the collection and sale of NTFPs.

Ingles et al (2006, p19) also argue that the project interventions 'provided a basis for further economic development through':

•   the establishment of an NTFP Marketing Group and NTFP Development Fund that:
    -   paid for improvements in formal and informal education
    -   provided credit in support of private equipment purchases and investments in agriculture, trading, transport and animal husbandry

- the substantial and robust increases in NTFP-based incomes that have allowed for private investments and livelihood diversification.

A potential methodological problem with participatory wealth ranking is that people may tell investigators what they think the investigators want to hear. The process may have minimized or eliminated this effect, as the rankings were carried out by a group of villagers and then reported to researchers. In any case, the use of a variety of different methods in the participatory exercise, including surveys and group discussions, was a way of verifying broad findings by triangulation (using consistent findings obtained by multiple methods).

Note

1 This case has been extracted (with minor modifications) from 'Bitter Bamboo and Sweet Living: Impacts of NTFP Conservation Activities on Poverty Alleviation and Sustainable Livelihoods. A Case Study of Lao PDR', a paper prepared for IUCN's 3I-C Project by Jason Morris, with research assistance by Sounthone Ketpanh, 2002. It has been revised and updated for the second edition of this book by Andrew Ingles.

Lessons for this book

- Conservation and poverty reduction can be achieved by removing constraints. The NTFP project supported the development of local institutional arrangements that enabled cooperation and better marketing. These new institutional arrangements transformed the potential (previously not fully utilized) asset, bamboo shoots, into an effectively realized asset. The project increased the capability of the villagers to achieve increased assets and reduce risks. In terms of the DFID framework, the institutional arrangement became a transforming structure.
- An adaptive learning approach is important. The project design was able to respond to a change in focus and a shift in implementation activities (such as the introduction of scales).
- It is possible to use a variety of methods such as participatory wealth ranking, surveys and household interviews to assess impacts of interventions on poverty.

Case Study 4
Ecosystem restoration and livelihoods in the Senegal River Delta, Mauritania[1]

O. Hamerlynck and S. Duvail

The context

Until the 1960s, the productivity of the Delta of the Senegal River was determined mainly by the annual flood and its mixing with salt water. Freshwater from the seasonal rainfall on the Fouta Djalon mountains in Guinea would traverse 1800 kilometres of drylands to reach the Delta in August, initially filling a network of channels and depressions. In October, hundreds of square kilometres (km[2]) of deltaic plains would be covered for weeks. At flood recession, pasture would sprout on the clay soils, attracting nomadic livestock keepers with their cattle and camels. The depressions would hold water until February–March and were exploited by resident fisherfolk and myriads of waterbirds. The Delta was one of the most important wintering grounds for Western Palearctic waterbirds, accommodating hundreds of thousands of ducks, waders and piscivorous birds. The mangrove and acacia forests offered nesting sites to tens of thousands of cormorants, herons, storks, spoonbills, etc. and were a nursery for marine fish (in particular mullets and shad) and for Penaeid shrimp. In favourable years, thousands of pelicans and two species of flamingo bred on islands in the depressions.

From the 1970s onwards, the Delta went through a series of crises. Across the Sahel, the drought of the 1970s and 1980s decimated livestock and forced the former nomadic populations to become sedentary. On the Mauritanian bank of the Delta these were predominantly Haratin, liberated slaves settling as small clan units in dispersed camps that gradually evolved into villages. Livelihoods remained essentially flood-dependent: fishing, hunting waterbirds, keeping small livestock, weaving mats using *Sporobolus* grasses and leather tanned with acacia seedpods. However, good floods became increasingly rare as the mean annual flow of the river decreased from about 800 cubic metres per second (between 1904 and 1970) to about 450 cubic metres per second (Bader et al, 2003). For cash, a substantial portion of the male population kept small shops across the border in Senegal's booming cities or went looking for labour opportunities in construction work or marine fisheries within Mauritania.

In the mid-1980s, the Senegal River basin agency OMVS (Organisation pour la mise en valeur du fleuve Sénégal) completed two dams: an 11 cubic kilometre storage dam upstream in Mali at Manantali and a salt-wedge dam downstream in the Delta at Diama (see Figure 3.1). The US$800million dams were designed to provide water for irrigated agriculture on 37,500km[2] of floodplain, produce 800GWh of hydropower, make the river navigable from the ocean to Mali and stop the dry season saltwater intrusion into the Delta. In spite of massive

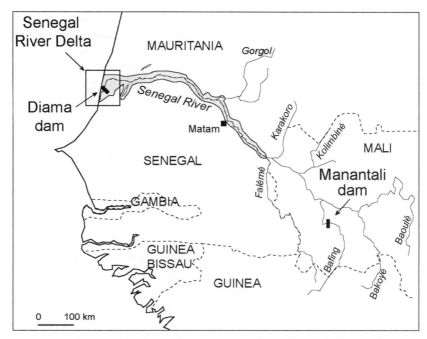

Figure 3.1 *Map of the Senegal River Basin, the Delta and the two dams*

Source: S. Duvail (2006).

additional donor investment over two decades (US$1500–6500 per hectare), only about 20 per cent of the planned irrigated area is cultivated annually (Fraval et al, 2002). High input and maintenance costs make rice cultivation in the floodplain inaccessible to the small-scale farmers who used to depend on recession agriculture. The official policy is that managed flood releases from Manantali permit recession agriculture to continue on 500km². Until irrigated agriculture catches on, however, flood support has rarely been adequate, neither spatially nor temporally as the single flood peak in October is often replaced by 'freak' releases from the dam, causing multiple peaks that flood areas already planted and result in crop losses. In the Delta, irrigation is not sustainable because of increasing soil salinity. Hydropower production started in 2002 and provides electricity to the three capitals of the OMVS member countries, Mali, Senegal and Mauritania. For the inhabitants of the Delta, however, the completion of the Diama reservoir in 1990 effectively eliminated the annual flooding that supported the ecosystem functions and their livelihoods. Moreover, the strong competition for irrigable land led to a border conflict between Senegal and Mauritania, causing the repatriation of the shopkeepers. All cross-border trade was stopped from 1989 to 1993.

In 1991, when Mauritania established the Diawling National Park (DNP) on

160km² of the 600km² deltaic floodplain (including the functionally dependent southernmost depressions of the Aftout es Saheli), the 900km² Lower Delta (including 300km² of dunes) had turned into a saline desert. Natural resource-based livelihoods and biodiversity had all but disappeared. Of about 15,000 residents less than 4000 remained, mainly women, children, the elderly and the infirm. Poverty was extreme in all its dimensions.

The intervention

From 1989 to 1999, with support from the Government of the Netherlands through DGIS, IUCN started collaborating with the Mauritanian Government on a rehabilitation plan for the Lower Delta in three successive phases (see Hamerlynck and Duvail, 2003). From the outset a participatory approach was favoured, in parallel with the introduction of more collaborative management of the adjacent Djoudj National Park in Senegal. In fact the history of the creation and extension of the Djoudj with forced resettlement and permanent conflict between forestry staff and local communities was well known on the Mauritanian side where the establishment of a protected area was less than welcome. It was necessary to prove that this would be a new type of protected area with solid guarantees for continued use by the local communities and a commitment towards the development of new sources of income. This model was in competition with a proposal by the rice-growing lobby for a vast irrigation project. In the first phase, before 1993, priority was given to livelihood support to women's groups, mainly for market gardening. This had become possible because of the permanent presence of freshwater in the Diama reservoir. Funds were also made available for the drafting of the necessary legal texts and the delimitation of park boundaries.

The second phase started in 1994 with an extensive consultation with the user communities (fisherfolk, livestock keepers, gatherers), which confirmed that the restoration of the pre-dam flood regime and the creation of an artificial estuary would be the most appropriate management for both the protected area and the adjacent floodplains. The emphasis of this phase was on the construction of 15 per cent of the hydraulic infrastructure (embankments, sluice gates). The outlay was only completed in 1999 with additional support from the French Development Agency and the African Development Bank. Sociological, economic and biophysical surveys were undertaken. Managed flood releases were practised from 1994 onwards, progressively inundating larger areas for longer time periods. The impact of each artificial flood on the natural resources and the livelihoods was monitored in collaboration with a multidisciplinary team from the University of Nouakchott, twinned with foreign students. Feedback discussions were held with each of the user groups that led to adaptations in the flood regime until a compromise scenario was reached (Duvail and Hamerlynck, 2003). The optimal scenario, as applied in the third phase since 1997, includes the need to apply some interannual variability in order to simulate the natural system more closely. In practice, this variability has been much larger than envisaged because of external contingencies such as the low priority accorded by OMVS to uses other than irrigation, wet season repairs to embankments and invasive aquatic plants from the Diama reservoir blocking the sluice gates.

A fourth phase, with the main outcome being the establishment of a transboundary biosphere reserve including the Djoudj and other protected areas of the Delta, is currently being implemented by IUCN and the Directorate General for International Cooperation (DGIS) of the Netherlands, with support from the Global Environmental Facility (GEF) France.

The project's main objectives were to arrive at joint management of the natural resources within the protected area and to support livelihoods around it, mainly by restoring ecosystem functioning. Traditional users were allowed to continue practising their sustainable methods of extraction during the flood season on one third of the DNP, the Bell Basin. In addition the entire park is accessible for dry-season grazing. Livelihood support was provided throughout the lifetime of the project. On-demand training was provided for new and traditional activities, for example the raw material for mat-making had been scarce for decades and the inexperienced young women were trained. For equipment (fishing nets, boats, gardening tools, seeds, sewing machines, etc.) the project provided the capital outlay to be reimbursed and reinvested through a rotational fund system. The building of the park headquarters, supported by the Government of Catalonia, and some of the infrastructure works provided a welcome opportunity for paid labour in the initial phases.

The results

In conjunction with a number of years (1994, 1995, 1999, 2000, 2001) of comparatively favourable local rainfall (over 250mm), the managed flood releases resulted in a spectacular rehabilitation of vegetation and fauna on the dunes and in the floodplain (Hamerlynck and Duvail, 2003). Annual and perennial vegetational cover increased tremendously and actually became visible on satellite imagery. Floodplain acacia and mangrove trees recolonized their original habitat. Floodplain fish and estuarine shrimp, mullet and shad returned to their spawning and nursery areas and crocodiles reappeared. The average number of wintering waterbirds increased from less than 6000 in 1992–1993 to over 60,000 in 1994 (see Figure 3.2). Large colonies of breeding waterbirds have re-established themselves, especially since the reflooding of the southern depressions of the Aftout es Saheli (Hamerlynck et al, 2005). Warthogs are now so abundant that a hunting lodge has been reopened to the north of the park, attracting European trophy hunters. From the fauna present in the 1960s, only lion and red-fronted gazelle have not reappeared, though hippopotamus and manatee are rare visitors.

From the livelihoods point of view, the restoration of ecosystem functions completely reversed the socio-economic trends. The monetary income that the

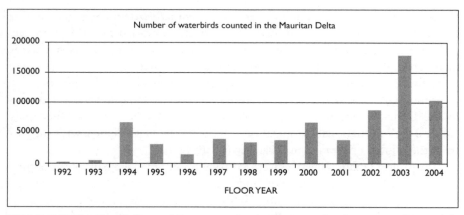

Figure 3.2 *Results of the mid-January waterbird counts for the area influenced by the managed flood releases by the DNP (Lower Delta and southern depressions of the Aftout es Saheli)*

Source: Diawling National Park

resident communities derive from the reflooding and the associated livelihood activities supported by the park stands at a minimum of US$780,000 per year (Moulaye, 2004). However, the value of local livestock production has probably been underestimated and nomadic livestock have not been taken into account in this calculation. Other produce (fisheries, gathering) exploited by non-residents has also been left out.

Fisheries, which after the completion of the Diama dam had declined to the point where only a handful of elderly men went out daily, have become a major source of income. The duration of the fishing season has been extended considerably and annual production has increased to about 300 tonnes. In the peak season (November–January), several dozen fishermen each earn over US$20 a day. Women have also benefited directly from the revival of this sector as they have started exporting fish to Senegal. Also, the renewed profitability of the fisheries is the main cause for the correction of the demographic imbalance that characterized the area; many young men are now permanent residents. The dominant tribe of fishermen, the Takhrédient, have authorized other local tribes to take up fishing and have allocated a prime fishing site to a neighbouring clan whose traditional fishing areas were about 30 kilometres upstream of the park. However, when the highly profitable prawn fisheries imported labourers from Senegal, they successfully affirmed their ancestral rights, supported by the DNP.

Mat-making, like most female activities in developing countries, is highly labour-intensive for a comparatively low profitability. In spite of the increased availability of raw material, the daily income from this activity stands at about US$0.60, but the number of women practising it has increased from a handful to several hundred, some coming from up to 50 kilometres away to harvest the *Sporobolus* grasses. Initially, this led to conflict as the newcomers were using less sustainable harvesting techniques. Through mediation by the DNP, all users have agreed to use the traditional methods. Because of indebtedness to the higher caste shopkeepers, the Haratin women sell their produce well below the market price.

Revenue from livestock keeping is difficult to evaluate. There is traditional secrecy about the size of the herds and a tendency for livestock to be used as a proxy of a savings account and therefore a tendency to sell fewer than would be economically 'optimal'. Also, milk products are very important in household consumption, especially for children, though this has not been quantified. Income is highly variable depending on the type of livestock kept, annual rainfall, mobility, etc. Still, nearly all households own a few small ruminants and the possession of a cow is perceived as a sign of affluence. Prior to the restoration, the total number of cattle owned by the resident population was about 50. Currently there are at least several hundred head, possibly over a thousand. In addition, several thousand head owned by nomadic tribes use the floodplains for dry-season grazing. In low rainfall years there is a lack of pasture on the dunes and resident and nomadic herds tend to converge on the edges of the floodplains before the vegetation has reached maturity and optimal biomass, negatively affecting the dry-season capacity. In the absence of alternative areas in the Delta, the DNP has very few means to counter this and with the general expansion of herds DNP suspects that over-grazing is becoming an issue.

Initially market gardening was an important source of income for the women's groups but, with the expansion of the activity all around the country, transport costs have become a constraint for the Delta and local markets are saturated early in the season. Relatively high input costs and the scarcity of land in proximity to an adequate freshwater supply have also led to a takeover of the most favourable areas by civil servants and the paramilitary. As the Delta is on one of the main migration routes to Europe, the labour force there is now predominantly foreign, West African and male. Income levels are around US$3 per day, comparable to what a schoolteacher would earn, but it is to be shared equitably between the 'owner' of the land and the labourer. In the more marginal areas, where market gardening is dependent on groundwater recharge from the floods, it is a seasonal activity that provides some income to women's groups, but transport and marketing are a major constraint.

In spite of considerable potential, tourism has not yet become a source of income for the local communities. Except for the desert and its oases in the north of the country, Mauritania is not a popular tourist destination. Many foreign tourists fly into northern Senegal and visit the Djoudj National Park or other protected areas in the Delta, but very few venture across the border. In the early days of the DNP, tour operators from St Louis quite successfully advertised the beautiful desert landscapes of the coastal dunes, the thrilling close-up views of large concentrations of flamingos and the exotic experience of having tea under a nomad tent. This initial success attracted a Mauritanian conglomerate to obtain a monopoly on all tourist transport and services. The local administration enforced the complex and expensive necessity of obtaining a visa even for a visit of a few hours only, unpredictable 'nuisance taxes' were created and have discouraged all initiative. A small number of birdwatchers and scientists visit the area but, not least because of the language barrier, they are guided by the park staff (for whom this is a welcome additional source of income) and not by the local communities.

The analysis

The structure and functions of the ecosystems of the Lower Delta and its associated livelihoods were annihilated by a combination of drought and dams. Still, a lot of damage could have been prevented by implementing the conservation and restoration measures prior to, or in conjunction with, dam construction. Fortunately, because of the extreme seasonality and the high interannual variability of the natural system, the surviving species are opportunistic and can react immediately to favourable conditions. The ecosystems are therefore resilient and, by simulating the annual flood, functions were comparatively easy to restore. The dams have in addition created the possibility of applying a near-optimal flood height each year and therefore the current management regime can be more productive than the natural system.

The protected area was highly controversial in its initial stages and the DNP authority has had to continuously prove the value of its management, be flexible and take local knowledge very seriously. Strategic mistakes such as the occasional lapse in the provision of reliable information to stakeholders are immediately punished with sabotage and non-cooperation. A clear majority of the local users has now adhered to the concept of a protected area with opportunities of sustainable resource use but many are disappointed by the slowness and the selective coverage of development interventions, such as drinking water supply and improved road access. Though planned, these have been delayed by issues of governance. Also, the DNP has sometimes created excessive expectations that remain a source of conflict. The DNP has been plagued by a high turnover of its trained staff and the performance of its local community development branch has been under par. One of the consequences of the high turnover of staff has been a less than optimal application of the management plan, leaving too much freshwater for too long in the upstream basins and not supplying enough to the artificial estuary. This increases the risk of vegetation changes with less nutritious sedges replacing the high quality pasture.

The protected area is in fact very small and covers only 160km^2, a third of which is permanently drowned in the reservoir and has become a virtually unexploited monoculture of the bulrush *Typha*. Satisfying all needs from such a small area is difficult. Fortunately the managed flood releases can positively affect about 500km² of floodplain, creating productivity at a much larger scale. Through groundwater recharge it even affects the adjacent dune systems and through the restoration of the nursery functions in the artificial estuary it probably impacts on other West African coastal wetlands such as the Banc d'Arguin and the fisheries-dependent livelihoods of the coastal population.

Local livelihoods were positively affected and the extreme monetary poverty that was ubiquitous in Lower Delta has to a large extent been eliminated by the opportunities offered through the restoration of the ecosystems and the accompanying local development measures. Still, over 70 per cent of the resident population can be characterized as poor on the basis of their habitat (tent or hut, no stone house) and their use of domestic energy (firewood, instead of gas, no artificial light), but account has to be taken of the generally frugal lifestyle inherited from the Moorish nomadic tradition. The structural poverty observed has many dimensions and, independently of natural resource abundance, is at least partially linked to the demographic dominance of the lowest caste of Mauritanian society, the Haratin. Their emancipation is a national issue and there are signs of change. Who would have expected that Haratin would become governors or ministers within a generation of the abolition of slavery in 1982? Today, two inhabitants of the Lower Delta have acceded to such posts. As able politicians they have attracted development projects to their home villages, resulting for example in electrification, improved access roads and drinking water supply. As individuals they have also become comparatively rich: they own large herds and motorized means of transport and have built stone houses with two floors. Through traditional solidarity their wealth trickles down to the clan and even 'upwards' to their impoverished high-caste tribal chiefs. Their livelihoods are largely independent of the local resources though their herds obviously benefit from the pasture provided by the restoration and they enjoy hunting. A few other inhabitants are also in the rich group, mainly high-level civil servants or successful businessmen and traders. Some of the livestock keepers are probably also affluent but hide it well.

About 25 per cent of the inhabitants are characterized as 'middle class'. They are mainly shopkeepers and traders who have resumed their activities in cities in Senegal and Mauritania. They often also own the local shops, buy the local produce and arrange transport to the markets and have benefited from the general resumption of economic activity in the Delta. Fisherfolk and some of the market gardeners have joined this comparatively well-to-do group and in their villages stone houses are quickly replacing the huts.

The 70 per cent of the population that is characterized as poor remains almost entirely dependent on the natural resources. There can be no doubt that their livelihoods have considerably improved through ecosystem restoration, an estimated US$1300 per household per year, but not enough to get them structurally out of poverty. This is especially true for the most vulnerable group,

the Haratin women, whose main source of income is mat-making but who are
indebted to the shopkeepers and therefore forced to sell cheap. A microcredit
system has recently been made available to the women's groups and the initial
results look promising.

Unfortunately, the managed flood releases can have little impact on the
southernmost 150km² of the Mauritanian Lower Delta. Thus the inhabitants of
the coastal dune around Ndiago and on the islands of Mboyo have not benefited
from the restoration efforts and only marginally from the development activities.
Also, the park has not been able to convince OMVS to practise properly timed
and adequate flood releases using the Diama dam. These could have had major
positive impacts on the southern Delta, at least prior to the creation of an artificial
breach in the coastal dune by the Senegalese authorities in 2003. This emergency
intervention to reduce the flood risk to the city of St Louis has shortened the
estuary and increased the tidal range downstream of the dam. Though this
has expanded the intertidal areas and seems to favourably affect the mangrove
(Hamerlynck et al, 2005), it has eliminated the annual flood and has negatively
affected the livelihoods of the inhabitants of the coastal dune. Because of the
reduced groundwater recharge, market gardening has collapsed and there is even
an acute drinking water crisis. Probably this breach will gradually close and move
southwards but the timescale of this evolution is at present unknown.

The future

The major worry for the sustainability of the intervention is the absence of a
mechanism for the internal financing of the maintenance and renewal costs of
the hydraulic infrastructure. All the embankments are constructed with local soft
substrates and their lifespan is limited to about ten years if well maintained. A
substantial proportion of the infrastructure is under the responsibility of OMVS
but the elements owned and managed by the park would need the setting aside of
about US$100,000 per year. This is only about 13 per cent of the annual monetary
surplus generated locally by the natural resources and could theoretically be
levied through access rights, especially if the nomadic herds would also be taxed.
However, any levy would conflict with the local perception of traditional user
rights.

A transboundary biosphere reserve was established in 2005 and it can be
hoped that this will favourably influence ecotourism by facilitating the border
crossing, for example waiving the visa requirement for visits of less than three
days. Currently hunting, birdwatching and cultural tourism in the Delta are the
monopoly of one of the largest industrial and agricultural conglomerates of the
country and very few benefits accrue to the local communities. At present tourism
does not contribute to infrastructure maintenance and renewal. Changing
this will require tough negotiations, a lot of local empowerment and capacity
building (guides, cooks) and investment in infrastructure (walkways, cycle paths,
accommodation).

On the basis of the 500km² strongly influenced by the managed flood releases, the investment in hydraulic infrastructure was only US$26 per hectare and the direct monetary benefit to the local users was at least US$1300 per affected household (or about US$150 per individual). There is still considerable potential to develop new livelihood opportunities, for example production of blue crabs for the restaurants of St Louis, increases in the proportion of revenue from mat-making accruing to the producers, and improvements to the governance of the injected conservation-development funds.

Comparatively easily and at a reasonable cost, the ecosystem restoration model could be expanded to other parts of the Delta and the Senegal River floodplain, especially to those parts of the Delta where irrigated rice has had to be abandoned because of the increase in soil salinity. Managed flood releases in those areas would reduce the livestock pressure on the DNP and open up livelihood opportunities upstream. With some adaptations, the DNP management model could probably also be combined with successful irrigated agriculture. This usually only exploits a small surface area of the floodplain while the rest is unnecessarily deprived of flooding.

Mauritania started producing offshore oil in 2006 and intensive exploration is also going on in the Delta. If successful, measures will need to be taken to minimize its potentially negative environmental and social impacts.

Note

1   The case study was commissioned for this book.

Lessons for this book

*   The restoration of ecosystem functioning can have positive benefits in terms of livelihoods and poverty reduction. In this case restoration was relatively easy due to the resilience of the natural environment, which was linked to the high degree of natural variability in the ecosystem.
*   The project illustrates the application of a landscape or ecosystem approach on a fairly large scale. The protected area is only a small part of the restored and managed area.
*   The ecosystem resulting from the intervention was not the same as the original natural system. In fact it was much more of a managed system and the authors argue that the construction of the dams, through regulating release of water, increased the productivity of the ecosystem. Despite the 'managed' nature of the ecosystem, biodiversity was considerably improved compared to the situation before the intervention.

Case Study 5
Association of Forest Communities of Petén, Guatemala[1]

Peter Leigh Taylor, Peter Cronkleton and Deborah Barry

Introduction

Since 1994, local communities have managed forest concessions in the Maya Biosphere Reserve in the Petén, Guatemala through their community-based associations (Gretzinger, 1998). With the assistance of their grassroots representative organization, the Association of Forest Communities of Petén (ACOFOP), these communities have produced significant positive outcomes of improved forest protection and social and economic benefits for their participants.

Guatemala's Petén region is recognized worldwide for its wealth of tropical biological diversity and its ancient Mayan archaeological sites. However, much like other high priority biodiversity 'hotspots' (Wilshusen et al, 2003), the Petén has been characterized by high levels of poverty, insecure land tenure and landlessness, unstable political systems and histories of military conflict. For many in the Petén, the intense competition among multiple interest groups to control the natural and cultural resources of Guatemala's most geographically and politically isolated region, compounded by a protracted civil war, created a state of 'ingovernability' in the region.

The Maya Biosphere Reserve (MBR) was established in northern Petén in 1990 as part of the United Nations' 'Man and Biosphere Programme' with over 2 million hectares of forest designated for varying levels of protection. The MBR's original territorial scheme defined a Nucleus Zone under strict preservation rules; a Multiple Use Zone (MUZ) representing about 50 per cent of the Reserve, and a buffer zone in which land and resource use was to be stabilized to relieve pressures on the MBR. Yet, as has often occurred elsewhere with protected areas (McShane, 2003), the planners of the MBR did not take adequate account of the complexity of pre-existing human settlement and livelihoods strategies dependent on natural resources. They also underestimated the degree of lawlessness and illegal extraction. Eviction, bans and other restrictions on access and resource use sparked conflict as local residents reacted to exclusion with resistance, including violence against reserve administration staff, destruction of vehicles and guard posts and kidnappings (Gómez and Méndez, 2005). For a government in peace negotiations in the mid-1990s aimed at ending a 30-year war, the results were creating an undesirable situation.

By promoting broader community involvement in forest management, the community concession system of the Petén was developed in large part as a way to mitigate conflict surrounding the MBR's administration and to address the government's own weak capacity to exercise control (Gómez and Méndez, 2005;

Monterosso and Barry, 2007). ACOFOP and its member community organizations have done much to bring 'governability' to the region's resource management. Unlike many experiences elsewhere, and despite ongoing obstacles and problems, this case suggests that conflict between biodiversity and development objectives need not lead to environmental degradation. Local communities can be effective resource stewards when there are avenues for meaningful participation in decision making, recognition of acquired rights, accompanied by fair distribution of costs and benefits of conservation as well as appropriate external support.

The policy context of conservation and development in Petén

The establishment and operation of the MBR has been a key piece of a larger international strategy of protected areas and reserves in Central America. As social conflict surrounding the MBR intensified, a debate emerged over how best to incorporate greater local participation in the reserve's operation. Influential participants in the debate included the Guatemalan government, bilateral and multilateral assistance agencies and international conservation organizations and the forest industrial sector (Monterroso and Barry, 2007). Though the forest industrial sector was considered, the decision makers opted for community concessions, albeit as Gómez and Méndez point out (2005), their support at first signalled more of an opposition to industrial concessions than a strong belief in local communities' capacities.

Twenty-five-year renewable forest management concession contracts were eventually granted to six communities and community-based groups in the MUZ, to six bordering the MUZ and to two local forest industries (Nittler and Tshinkel, 2005). The community concession system was an important innovation in the region, as it clearly laid out the rights of land and resource access, extraction, use, exclusion and even management for participating communities. Over a relatively short period of time, communities were given use and decision-making rights over large forest areas. The concession rights encompass both timber and NTFPs. For timber, a strict regulatory framework was established requiring the communities to gain international certification of their timber within a stipulated time period. Complex and detailed management plans were elaborated with substantial support from subsidized technical assistance and submitted to and approved by the National Commission on Protected Areas (CONAP). Once a community concession area was approved, for example, a forest inventory was carried out and management plans and environmental impact assessments developed. Five-year management plans and annual operating plans defined timber cutting schedules and cycles, annual allowable cuts, commercial species to be harvested, minimum cutting diameters, silvicultural treatments including liberation thinning, and protection strategies (CONAP, 1994, cited in Gretzinger 1998, p116). Until recently, concessionaires' activities have been mostly dedicated to commercial timber activities, although they have a long history of informal extraction of NTFPs such as decorative palm (*Chamaerdorea elegans, C. oblongata and C. ernesti-augustii*), chicle gum (*Manilkara* spp.) and allspice (*Pimenta doica*) (Taylor, 2007).

The role of the secondary-level association of community organizations has been a key element for success. ACOFOP first emerged in 1995, organized by community-based groups seeking forest management rights. Its objective was to improve 'the standard and quality of life of the Petén's forest communities, through sustainable management of the forest's resources' (ACOFOP, 2005). ACOFOP was a central player in the negotiation of communities' rights to manage the forest, as it represented the interests of first a few pioneers and finally 22 community organizations as a single interlocutor. The grassroots organization has also played a crucial role in opening up and defending space for communities to develop capacities for greater autonomy in management of the concessions.

International donors and conservation institutions played a crucial role early on in establishing fruitful dialogue on conservation and development and promoting the inclusion of community actors. Principal donors included the United States Agency for International Development (USAID), the World Bank, the German Kreditanstalt für Wiederaufbau (KFW), DFID and the Ford Foundation. USAID alone invested some US$50 million in Petén during 1990–2004 in support of CONAP, protected area management and technical support to the community concession organizations. USAID also promoted the involvement of international conservation organizations such as Conservation International and the Nature Conservancy who became the principal channels of technical service provision to CONAP and the community organizations. The Ford Foundation and Interchurch Organisation for Development Co-operation (ICCO), The Netherlands provided over US$1 million directly to ACOFOP and the community organizations between 1999 and 2006 to help increase their institutional capacity and advocacy skills.

Technical support was provided to the MBR and the community concession system through two approaches for development assistance. A traditional 'official' approach involved large-scale donor projects that effectively mobilized significant financial resources, helped develop legal and bureaucratic frameworks, supported infrastructure investment, recruited major international institutions to support resource management, and trained national officials. At the same time, a smaller scale, more process-oriented 'pro-community' model of assistance (Gómez and Méndez, 2005) aimed to help create conditions through which the forest communities could become highly proactive participants in shaping the model for community participation in conservation and development. It focused more on generating processes of learning and appropriation and ownership that could be sustained locally once external support was withdrawn.

This second model of assistance emerged over time through the communities' experience with external technical and financial support. First, the original concessions were far smaller than today, and the concession holders' role was initially intended to be more stewards and guardians of the forest areas. The community organizations through ACOFOP lobbied to expand the concession size. Community interest in expanding their role in timber management combined with recommendations from USAID consultants – influenced by experiences in neighbouring Mexico – together changed the model and took the project to a much larger scale in the region (Monterroso and Barry, 2007). The original concession contracts required communities to sign exclusive technical assistance contracts with local NGOs, which had been created by the larger international conservation organizations. These international NGOs and their national counterparts in many ways played a positive role. They helped communities satisfy legal and bureaucratic requirements to gain concession rights. They carried out socio-economic and technical planning and provided training and support for management and marketing (Gómez and Méndez, 2005).

However, the relationships between communities and the NGOs, according to many community members and observers, were often characterized by paternalism and dependency. Notably, NGOs were staffed by conservation experts (rather than forestry extension professionals) with little expertise in forestry, community development or business skills. ACOFOP and its associated communities and organizations complained that the NGOs' methodology did not allow communities to develop their own capabilities for integrated forest management, administration and business. From their perspective, with few exceptions, the external investment in assistance was rarely oriented 'toward the strengthening and training of the communities or ACOFOP in financial and administrative management' (Gómez and Méndez, 2005, p19).

Under pressure from ACOFOP, including international internet-based campaigns, and eventually crucial support from USAID itself, this obligatory NGO model was ended in 2001. USAID began directly relating to the community concessions in 2002, emphasizing reduction of subsidies, strengthening of business management and reduction of assistance agencies (Gómez and Méndez, 2005). Communities gained greater freedom to seek technical assistance that they felt would be adequate to meet their needs, as long as the assistance complied with the technical requirements of the concession contracts. Several NGOs continue today to provide technical assistance to the concessions, though on terms more acceptable to communities. Today, some of ACOFOP's associated members operate a community-owned forest services firm, FORESCOM, through which they obtain support for forest certification procedures and timber commercialization (Gómez and Méndez, 2005). ACOFOP itself, and many of the associated community organizations and enterprises, have acquired significant technical expertise that over time has changed their relations with external technical service providers.

Currently, ACOFOP has 23 affiliated communities and associations, directly representing about 2000 individual members. Its affiliates include indigenous and mostly *ladino* (mixed ethnic descent) communities, and a range of organizations including not-for-profit cooperatives and for-profit associations. The number of members of each associated group ranges from 10 to over 400, with concession areas ranging from 350 to over 80,000 hectares (ACOFOP, 2005; Tropico Verde, 2005). ACOFOP has itself evolved into an 'indigenous technical assistance' provider, fielding its own modest extension staff in the communities, helping coordinate and channel external support to its members. Perhaps most significantly, ACOFOP has played a key role in direct political representation of its members in national and international arenas where external decisions are made that affect the Petén's natural resources and its communities.

Poverty reduction impacts

Little systematic data is yet available on the MBR and community concessions' direct contributions to poverty reduction, particularly at the household level. Nevertheless, in the Petén preliminary indications are that the community concessions are producing significant positive social and economic benefits for participating communities. Nittler and Tschinkel's (2005) evaluation, for example, found that the concessions generated US$5 million annually in wood products and US$2–3 million in NTFPs. In 2003, they generated more than 50,000 person days of work with a value of nearly US$360,000. ACOFOP has reported that the concessions directly and indirectly benefit up to 14,000 individuals in 30 communities. ACOFOP also observes that its members' forest concessions generated significant tax revenue for the Guatemalan government, estimated at US$424,000 in 2003 (ACOFOP, 2004).

Additional systematic research is currently under way on the concession system's social and economic impacts for its members, in some cases including the extent to which benefits reach beyond participating members to non-member residents in local communities. More in-depth work needs to be done to understand the social, economic and political benefits the concession system has brought to the region.

Biodiversity and conservation impacts

Reliable time series data on the conservation impacts of ACOFOP's associated community concessions is limited but recently analysed evidence shows significant positive impacts, particularly when the concession areas are compared to neighbouring parks and MUZs managed by government institutions and NGOs and which have suffered high levels of forest cover loss from burning, logging and other illegal activities (Nittler and Tschinkel, 2005; Bray et al, Forthcoming). Satellite monitoring studies commissioned by conservation groups in collaboration with CONAP indicate dramatic positive impacts in concession areas on fire reduction, deforestation and illegal extraction (Wildlife Conservation Society et al, 2003, 2004). A biological monitoring study found that logging appears not to have posed a major threat to ecological integrity in the Reserve (Radachowsky, 2004).

Another study of the cultural impact of the concession suggests that the community concession holders are carrying out good faith efforts to protect archaeological sites. The study's authors recommend that a cultural management system similar to the community forest concessions be explored to protect the region's cultural resources (Roney et al, undated).

Despite these positive indications, more systematic evaluation of the concessions' impact on conservation and biodiversity protection in the Petén is needed, including analysis of additional factors such as colonization history and variations in demographic pressures (David Bray, personal communication).

Sustainability of the concession system

Organizational design and capacity have been important keys to the community concessions' significant success in developing sustainable forest management. Established and developed through deliberation (sometimes conflictual) and with crucial support from external assistance agencies, the concessions and ACOFOP themselves are now developing a growing level of autonomy and protagonism in sharp contrast to many subsidized forest community groups elsewhere. During this stage of community concession development they have emerged as a recognized and important actor in the region. The great challenge of the community concessions is to consolidate, deepen and extend that capacity for the longer term. Yet in doing so, they face significant challenges from both internal and external sources.

Internally, some community concessions are suffering from significant resource management problems. Four concessions in the San Andrés area, according to ACOFOP and CONAP staff, are experiencing significant biodiversity losses because of agricultural burning and land-use change for ranching. These concessions have historically weaker organizations, their members originally came from agrarian communities, they received some of the least commercially valuable forests, and must contend with anomalous large private landholdings within their concessions that do not follow the MBR's conservation rules. Nevertheless, the problems of these concessions serve as focal points for external criticism of the concession system and threaten to undermine external support for the majority of the concessions that are doing well (Nittler and Tschinkel, 2005; Taylor, 2007).

Another source of internal pressure stems from growing tensions between concession members and non-members in concession communities (Tropico Verde, 2005; Taylor, 2007). The community concessions were originally granted to communities and groups of community members who had organized to petition CONAP for forest management rights. Not all community members became involved at the beginning as they lacked experience with or interest in timber management. But as forest management-related activities and income have grown, new tensions have emerged between those with legal management rights and those without those rights. Critics of the community concessions argue that the economic benefits of the concessions are not sufficient to significantly change living conditions, even in a strong concession community such as Carmelita. Moreover, economic benefits have been limited almost exclusively to concession members and, therefore, the concessions represent a *de facto* privatization of the MUZ (Tropico Verde, 2005). Nevertheless, many of the concession activities, such as sawmills and carpentry shops, have generated jobs and other benefits for non-members. The internal statutes of many concessions moreover require investment of a proportion of net returns in projects benefiting the community as a whole (though these rules are not always consistently followed) (Nittler and Tschinkel, 2005). Notwithstanding, pressure grows on ACOFOP and its associated concessions to find a way to extend forest management concessions and benefits to non-members. This tension highlights the reality that Petén's communities are not homogeneous but are populated by internal groups holding distinct interests and perspectives on the region's resources. It also reveals the necessity for organizational models to be flexible and adapt to changing conditions.

Externally, communities' rights to participate in forest management face continued pressure in a context in which natural and cultural resource conservation and development are shaped by powerful external actors. Numerous efforts have been marshalled in recent years by petroleum companies to expand exploration and exploitation in community concession areas. Thus far, ACOFOP and its members have successfully opposed these incursions on their resource rights. However, the recent case of the proposal to expand the Mirador Basin protected area in northern Petén underscores the continued pressures, particularly those related to tourism, that pose major threats to the concessions.

In 2003, the US-based Foundation for Anthropological Research and the Global Heritage Fund proposed to expand the area surrounding the Mirador cultural site to include the Mirador-Rio Azul National Park, the Naachatún-Dos Lagunas Biotope and parts of six community forest concessions. This area is said to contain one of the most important Mayan temples in the region, and is intended to become the centrepiece of a large-scale tourism investment. The plan's proponents argued that illegal hunting, logging and archaeological theft threatened the area's wealth of biodiversity and cultural treasures. Opponents, including ACOFOP, its concession members and their supporters, argued that the plan would bypass MBR laws and regulations and unduly affect or halt legitimate concession activities. Moreover, they argued that the plan's tourism development strategy would bring new and unacceptable pressures on the forest and its resources. Though the plan had significant high-level Guatemalan support, in mid-2005 it was overturned by the nation's Supreme Court. External pressure to develop Petén's cultural resources continues, including the recent proposed declaration of the region as a global Cultural Heritage site, and new projects to develop access to Mirador via the Carmelita concession.

Today, in response to its own significant success, emerging internal tensions and continued external pressures, ACOFOP and its members are seeking to move beyond commercial timber extraction to develop a more diversified but integrated management approach including NTFPs and services such as *xate* (jade palm), *chicle* (natural gum), community-based eco-tourism and cultural site protection. They hope that this more diversified approach will help consolidate the community concessions for the future, responding to conservationist concerns about timber exploitation and opening up new opportunities for both concession members and non-members (Taylor, 2007).

In addition, together with ACOFOP, community concessions are considering alternative tenure models that could provide longer term security of resource access and help maintain sustainable use. The concession system within the MBR is bound by official commitments to a model that combines conservation and sustainable management. Concessionaires and conservationists alike have registered increasing social pressure on land in the surrounding areas of the MBR, mostly for conversion to agriculture and ranching. Some fear that the future government may opt for diminishing the size, role and regulations based on conservation in favour of expanding the agricultural frontier and developing tourism. If this were to occur, the large forested areas protected by communities could become areas of rapid speculation and land grabs. Though hopefully thwarted by concerted collective action, this possible trend has led communities to begin to explore alternative tenure arrangements that would allow them to have more secure rights over the concession land and forests.

The community concessions of the Petén need appropriate technical assistance to consolidate and extend their achievements and address their weaknesses. Priority needs include developing appropriate new productive activities, designing related organizational models and adjusting their legal status accordingly, establishing new market linkages and enhancing organizational capacity for negotiation with external stakeholders. Ideally, technical assistance would combine the strengths of traditional 'official' assistance with those of alternative 'pro-community' support. The official model is better suited to making possible larger-scale coordinated investments in the physical, legal and policy infrastructure of sustainable management for conservation and development. The pro-community model is more flexible, process-oriented and better suited to building local organizational capacity. The two approaches can be complementary.

Note

1   Except where otherwise noted, this case study is largely based on two reports emerging from the 'Assistance to Grassroots Forestry Organizations' project of the Center for International Forestry Research funded by the Ford Foundation (Cronkleton et al, 2008; Taylor et al, 2008).

Lessons for this book

- Community forestry frequently focuses on income generation through NTFPs. This case demonstrates the potential of commercial timber production by communities, often ignored or assumed to be too difficult.
- The case demonstrates the potential of a community-based approach to concessions.
- Business and marketing expertise, in addition to conservation and technical forestry expertise, are among the most pressing needs for participants in community forest management. Such expertise is not always present in supporting organizations and agencies.
- The development of communities' capacity to act as protagonists in decision making related to Petén's natural and cultural resources has been crucial. Community-based associations at the local and secondary levels have been key to effective empowerment. As a grassroots-based political organization forged during the process of organizing the concessions and effectively representing a diverse array of communities, community-based organizations and productive strategies, ACOFOP has played a key role in developing the political capacities of concession holders. ACOFOP has also become an effective interlocutor between local people and external agencies and stakeholder groups. Sustaining its role over time, however, is a challenge, because new emerging organizations restructure the governance of the area.

4

Scale, Landscapes, Boundaries and Negotiation

Introduction

Chapter 2 looked at previous approaches to combining poverty issues with conservation and their limited success in terms of benefits to people. It also noted some concepts that may be useful in understanding the linkages between poverty and conservation. The case studies in Chapter 3 explored ways in which poverty and conservation issues have been addressed. These two chapters provide the context for a discussion of a reinvigorated approach to sustainable development, one that ensures that both conservation and poverty reduction are addressed explicitly. Sustainable development is the ideal objective, however difficult it may be to achieve in practice.

The word 'reinvigorated' is used deliberately; we do not claim to promote a completely new approach. Valuable work has been done through ICDPs and community-based natural resource management programmes and projects.

Our approach builds on many of the concepts and achievements of earlier initiatives. Terminology is always a problem in development thinking. Good ideas need a label but these labels come to be associated with particular concepts and experiences, often becoming more rigid than was originally intended. (Broad descriptive labels also get reduced to acronyms.) ICDPs are a case in point. It is easier to invent a new term than it is to redefine an old one. It is for this reason that we have avoided adopting a label in the form of a catchphrase. Whatever term is selected, it would ultimately need to be replaced with a new term representing new thinking. The important thing is not the term but the broad range of elements it describes.

This chapter explores some of the key issues in implementing approaches that link poverty reduction and conservation. Chapter 5 continues the discussion, paying particular attention to ways of incorporating the institutional context into poverty reduction and conservation.

Linkages and trade-offs

Much of the discussion about ICDPs and similar approaches has centred on the extent to which conservation and development objectives are compatible. This involves questions about trade-offs between conservation and development and creating linkages.

It has often been argued that development is in conflict with conservation. A competing view holds that conservation and development are complementary. This is sometimes associated with the view that conservation is impossible – or at least difficult – without meeting peoples' needs. This position is the basis of integrated conservation and development approaches. It has led to the proposition that meeting peoples' needs is an important step in achieving conservation and that, in pragmatic terms, obtaining the cooperation and support of people is essential to achieving conservation.

The pragmatic argument for seeking peoples' involvement has several aspects:

- The essentially economic argument states that people may change behaviours that damage the environment through overexploitation if they are able to meet their needs by other means, including through alternatives sources, through incentives and through changing behaviour to implement sustainable practices.
- People often have knowledge, skills and organizational capacities that are useful in resource management and local knowledge is particularly useful and relevant. This notion of local capacities is evident in the current literature on indigenous or local knowledge.
- People are more likely to follow resource management agreements and rules if they have had input into these agreements. Participation in decision making makes it more likely that the agreements will meet their needs and will reflect what is achievable.

A wealth of evidence supports the view that rural communities have the capacity to manage natural resources sustainably (see for example the cases of Pred Nai mangrove forest in Thailand, Case Study 1, and forest restoration in Shinyanga in Tanzania, Case Study 2). However, indigenous conservation should not be romanticized. Communities sometimes do lack the capacity or desire to manage resources sustainably and frequently are unable to deal with external constraints that limit their capacity. Nevertheless, such capacities are common, if not always present, and represent an enormous opportunity if appropriately recognized and supported.

Seeking the best possible outcomes

Chapter 2 pointed out that ICDPs have not been very effective in addressing human livelihood needs and poverty concerns. Other programmes that attempt to meet livelihoods and conservation needs (such as community forestry, joint forest management and so on) have also had limited success in improving livelihoods (Fisher, 2003). Some conservationists argue that integrated projects have failed even to achieve conservation goals; Chapter 2 discussed critiques of ICDPs by Oates (1999) and Barrett and Arcese (1995).

Attempting to return to a concept of conservation as preservation is probably impractical in terms of the financial, political and social costs. Integration of conservation and development must be made to work both for practical and ethical reasons. This position is not based on romantic ideas about communities in harmony with nature. Nor is it based on undue optimism about win–win outcomes.

An integrated approach will not necessarily achieve perfect outcomes in terms of conservation or development. In fact, perfect biodiversity outcomes are often impossible under realistic day-to-day conditions. In the case of the Pred Nai community mangrove project (Chapter 3), for example, the result is not a mangrove with 'pristine' biodiversity values. The biodiversity, however, is far greater than it was before the community became involved in protection and management. Linking conservation and poverty reduction means trying to achieve the best possible outcome, not necessarily a perfect outcome. But while win–win situations are not always possible, they are not as uncommon as is sometimes asserted. Rather than thinking in terms of win–win, win–lose or lose–lose combinations, it may be more useful to think in terms of win-more–lose-less (William Sunderlin, CIFOR, personal communication).

It is important to remember that the outcomes of community-based activities should not be judged by higher standards than those that apply to possible and realistic alternatives or by standards that alternative methods have been unable to achieve. For example, although it could be argued that many community forests in Nepal are not highly biodiverse, they often exhibit much greater biodiversity than the degraded landscapes that existed when they were formally under government control. There is no reason to think that a return to management by the forest department would lead to any improvement. Indeed, one reason why the forest department took on community forestry in the first place is precisely because it recognized that it did not have the capacity to achieve effective forest management on the scale required without community support.

Although much of the debate about conservation and development focuses on areas with high conservation values – protected areas or potential protected areas – conservation is not just about protected areas. It also relates to multi-use landscapes, degraded landscapes and many other areas where conservation values and poverty/livelihood issues exist. And although addressing poverty issues may be particularly difficult in protected areas and areas of high biodiversity, it may be easier elsewhere. Debate should not be framed only by extreme and difficult cases. Different approaches need to be developed for different situations. Some broad principles will remain the same (including ethical principles), but specifics will vary.

Conceptual tools for addressing conservation and poverty reduction

Two elements can contribute in a major way to conservation and poverty reduction:

1   When assessing causes of poverty and degradation and opportunities for poverty reduction and conservation, it is important to look beyond the local level to multiple geographical scales and institutional levels. This includes building opportunities through an ecosystem approach and, more broadly, considering institutional contexts and opportunities. This chapter explores these questions of scale.
2   Poverty should be seen not just in terms of the absence of assets and resources, but as a lack of capability to realize the benefits of these assets. This involves focusing on 'transforming structures and processes' (as they are called in the DFID livelihood framework). These structures and processes turn the various forms of capital (or 'assets' according to the World Bank) into livelihood outcomes. They include marketing systems (for example for income generation based on NTFPs), tenure reform and policy changes, and are often institutional in nature (see Chapter 5).

Multiple scales and multiple levels

Although ecologists and conservationists have long recognized that issues affecting conservation are frequently not site-specific but sometimes occur at remote locations, they often continue to focus on site-specific action. Further, the root causes of biodiversity loss are frequently not physical but rather political, social or economic, and these underlying causes occur at a variety of scales. If biodiversity conservation is to be effective, action needs to occur at different scales and locations. A similar point applies to poverty. The underlying causes of poverty tend to be found at a variety of levels, not just locally. Acknowledging these concepts helps us understand the limits of site-level approaches to both conservation and poverty reduction and provides an opportunity to link conservation and poverty reduction.

The ecosystem approach

During the 1990s the ecosystem approach emerged as 'a strategy for the management of land, water and living resources that promotes conservation and sustainable use in an equitable way' (Smith and Maltby, 2003, pi). The ecosystem approach has become widely accepted and in May 2000 it was endorsed by the fifth Conference of the Parties to the Convention on Biological Diversity (CBD) as an approach to implement the Convention.

The ecosystem approach recognizes sustainable use, accepts that change is inevitable, argues that objectives are socially constructed and subject to multiple interests and includes concerns with devolved management. Thus, in many ways it is consistent with poverty reduction and conservation. The principles of the ecosystem approach are set out in Box 4.1.

Shepherd (2004) has developed a five-step approach to implementing the ecosystem approach in the field. The 12 principles are clustered 'into a logical sequence which encourages discussion, planning and a step-by-step approach' (Shepherd, 2004, p1). This guide to implementation stresses the importance of adaptive management as a way to deal with 'unforeseen negative impacts' and 'unforeseen issues'. These are the five steps (Shepherd, 2004, p3):

> *Step A: Determining the main stakeholders, defining the ecosystem area,*
> *and developing the relationship between them*
> *Step B: Characterising the structure and function of the ecosystem, and*
> *setting in place mechanisms to manage and monitor it*
> *Step C: Identifying the important economic issues that will affect the*
> *ecosystem and its inhabitants*
> *Step D: Determining the likely impact of the ecosystem on adjacent*
> *ecosystems*
> *Step E: Deciding on long-term goals, and flexible ways of reaching them*

Box 4.1 Principles of the ecosystem approach

Principle 1   The objectives of management of land, water and living resources are a matter of societal choice.

Principle 2   Management should be decentralized to the lowest appropriate level.

Principle 3   Ecosystem managers should consider the effects (actual or potential) of their activities on adjacent and other ecosystems.

Principle 4   Recognizing potential gains from management, there is usually a need to understand and manage the ecosystem in an economic context. Any such ecosystem-management programme should:

    a)   Reduce those market distortions that adversely affect biological diversity;

    b)   Align incentives to promote biodiversity conservation and sustainable use; and

    c)   Internalize costs and benefits in the given ecosystem to the extent feasible.

Principle 5   Conservation of ecosystem structure and functioning, in order to maintain ecosystem services, should be a priority target of the ecosystem approach.

Principle 6   Ecosystems must be managed within the limits of their functioning.

Principle 7   The ecosystem approach should be undertaken at the appropriate spatial and temporal scales.

Principle 8   Recognizing the varying temporal scales and lag-effects that characterize ecosystem processes, objectives for ecosystem management should be set for the long term.

Principle 9   Management must recognize that change is inevitable.

Principle 10   The ecosystem approach should seek the appropriate balance between, and integration of, conservation and use of biological diversity.

Principle 11   The ecosystem approach should consider all forms of relevant information, including scientific and indigenous and local knowledge, innovations and practices.

Principle 12   The ecosystem approach should involve all relevant sectors of society and scientific disciplines.

Source: Smith and Maltby (2003)

The landscape concept

A supportive concept to the ecosystem approach, known as the landscape concept or landscape perspective, has emerged. Some people prefer the concept of landscape instead of ecosystems, feeling that the word 'ecosystem' tends to imply a primary focus on biophysical factors. This is not the intention of proponents of ecosystem management, who make it clear 'that people are an integral part of ecosystems' (Pirot et al, 2000, pxi) and that ecosystem management is about sustainable management for human use. The word 'landscape' is much more readily seen as relating to human landscapes. We see the landscape concept as being a subset of, and complementary to, the ecosystem approach.

Maginnis et al (2004) argue that conventional land-use planning tends to be based on the 'problem isolation paradigm', which breaks down complex problems into discrete components and deals with each component separately. The problem is that land-use problems do not exist in isolation. Trying to achieve conservation by maintaining species in isolated areas, however large, rarely works:

> *Just as biodiversity cannot be contained within the confines of a protected area, neither people (nor economic development) can easily be kept out of areas required for the conservation of biodiversity (areas that may, but usually do not, coincide with the boundaries of national parks). (Maginnis et al, 2004, p323)*

The landscape concept has been proposed as an alternative to this type of thinking in terms of fragmented land-use zones. Maginnis et al (2004, p331) define a landscape as 'a contiguous area, intermediate in size between an "ecoregion" and a "site", with a specific set of ecological, cultural and socioeconomic characteristics distinct from its neighbours'.[1] It is important to emphasize that it is the set that is distinctive, not any single characteristic.

Landscapes consist of adjacent locations under different forms of land use. An underlying idea is that the whole is more than the sum of its parts. Another important point is that boundaries are essentially arbitrary; they are defined by people for a particular purpose. In practice, landscapes based on different boundaries defined for different people often overlap and are often permeable. It is possible to think of a number of landscapes superimposed upon each other. These could include land use, cultural, economic or political landscapes as well as conservation landscapes.

An example of a landscape might be an area with a number of different land uses, such as scattered forest patches, a larger area of forest that functions as a wildlife refuge, private farming areas, grazing lands used by migratory pastoralists and wetlands used by local fisherfolk. Recognizing the physical characteristics of the terrain is one thing, although defining the boundaries between it and similar adjoining areas may be difficult. Superimposed on the physical landscape are different social categories. There are several villages with discreet but informal boundaries within the landscape. All of the area falls within a single administrative (local government) unit, but it comprises only a part of the unit and administrative headquarters are located outside. The grazing land is used seasonally by pastoralists, whose grazing area includes separate areas outside the landscape. The boundaries are permeable; both people and wild animals move beyond them.

Selection of criteria for drawing boundaries depends on the objectives of those doing the drawing. Given that boundaries are, in a sense, arbitrary, why are they where they are? Perhaps a particular area has been chosen for land-use planning. Alternatively, the area may be dominated by people from a particular ethnic group, different from those in surrounding areas. Thus there is a conservation landscape as well as overlapping cultural and livelihood landscapes. From the point of view of intervention, the important thing is not which boundaries are selected, but that we think in terms of a landscape perspective involving a number of interconnected sites with varying functions. The boundaries will always remain fuzzy.

The landscape concept is highly relevant to attempts to deal with poverty reduction and conservation objectives. One of the key concepts in providing income and livelihoods from natural resources is the idea of multiple use. Although it may be difficult to achieve multiple use while increasing or maintaining biodiversity at the site level, the landscape level will often provide far more opportunities. Different parts of the landscape can be used to achieve different results. One purpose of the landscape concept is to balance net energy flows at the landscape level rather than the site level. The aim is to meet various objectives (such as food production, income generation, maintenance of forest cover) for the landscape as a whole, not for each specific site.

Application to poverty reduction and conservation

The ecosystem approach and landscape concept are useful ways to look at conservation issues spatially beyond the site level and also helpful in identifying opportunities to balance site-level trade-offs in an equitable way. Spatial issues do not stop at the landscape level, however, and sometimes the physical causes of conservation threats occur in remote locations.

Examples include cases where upstream pollution (often hundreds of kilometres away) affects river ecology and fisheries, or situations where residue from agricultural chemicals and sediments discharged by coastal streams affects offshore coral reefs, as is the case of the Great Barrier Reef in Australia and in the Caribbean. Sometimes the threats to conservation and livelihoods arise in a different country, as in the case of the Yali Falls Dam (see Box 4.2).

Geographically distant causes are not the only type of remote causes. Policy in one country can easily have a major impact in other countries. For example, logging bans in Thailand and China have led to increased logging and forest loss in Lao PDR, Cambodia, Indonesia, the Russian far east and Mongolia. The resultant commercial logging may have both positive and negative effects on local livelihoods, providing employment but reducing access to land for agriculture and rights to use forest land. This type of issue needs to be dealt with at the level of international negotiations.

Thus, multiple scales are not just a matter of ever-widening geographical

Box 4.2 The Yali Falls Dam and transboundary effects

The Yali Falls Dam is located on the Se San River in Vietnam. Rural people living downstream in Ratanakiri Province, Northeast Cambodia, have experienced serious negative effects from the dam. A study (DOF and NTFP Project, 2000) showed that the Yali Falls Dam (part of a hydroelectric scheme) caused changes in water levels and quality, which had major impacts on the downstream population. Approximately 20,000 people have been affected.

Flooding destroyed crops and villages and disrupted economic activities (including fishing, food gathering and gold-panning). It also caused riverbank erosion. According to the report, a number of people were drowned and nearly a thousand people died from diseases attributed to declining water quality. The ecological effects included a declining fish population, which in turn was blamed for reduced fish catches.

Source: Based on DOF and NTFP Project (2000)

scales, but also include an institutional and political landscape that can be thought of as a vertical dimension. In other words, we need to think both of *multiple institutional levels* and *multiple geographical scales*. The way in which food security is defined in Lao PDR (see Box 4.3) illustrates the ways in which poverty and conservation at site levels are affected by institutional factors such as policy. In this case, policy focuses on food security through rice production, whereas human livelihoods depend substantially on fisheries associated with wetlands. In fact, it is really a wetlands economy, not a rice economy. Policy interventions based on an inaccurate understanding of local livelihoods can be counterproductive.

We propose a conceptual framework for analysing causal connections between processes at different locations and at different institutional levels. It is a context for analysis and understanding, as well as a framework for action. This multi-scale and multilevel analysis identifies where problems arise and, by extension, where to act for improvement. There is no point in trying to solve a problem at the site level if the immediate or underlying causes of that problem are off-site or operate at another level.

One reason that ICDPs and other attempts to integrate conservation and poverty objectives have not worked well in the past is that they tend to focus too much on action at the site level. This may be partly because of the understandable tendency to see conservation issues as occurring at physical sites. The failure of many project-level interventions in conservation – and in development generally – is partly related to this failure to address causes at other levels.

Considering multiple geographical scales and multiple institutional levels has serious implications in terms of how interventions should be targeted:

- Since factors affecting poverty and conservation operate at multiple levels and scales, attempts to address problems must also do so. Solutions should have multiple points of entry.
- It is not necessary for any single programme or project to deal with all relevant levels, but alliances need to be made to ensure that all relevant levels are being addressed by somebody.
- Interventions at all levels need to be linked 'upwards' and 'downwards' (in terms of both geographical scale and institutional level) to other interventions.

Box 4.3 Understanding poverty in rural Lao PDR

Although there are many categories of poverty in Lao PDR, with different causes and characteristics, officially poverty is largely defined in terms of rice deficit. An important rural development strategy, therefore, is to increase rice production. This is done through cultivating new lowland areas, particularly wetlands and floodplains, promoting irrigation of a second crop and to some extent promoting intensification of production.

However, rice deficit is not always the same as nutritional deficit. Although cultivation of rice is a fundamental economic and livelihood activity in Lao PDR, most rural people depend on a wide range of natural goods, particularly wild resources available from common property wetlands, rivers and forests. These wild resources often provide important nutrition that cannot be provided by rice alone. While rice deficits are common in many parts of Lao PDR, the ability to cope with these deficits and maintain reasonable nutritional status depends on being able to harvest these wild resources.

In order to address these issues, IUCN, in partnership with the Food and Agriculture Organization (FAO) and the Living Aquatic Resources Research Centre (LARReC) in Lao PDR, undertook a participatory assessment of the role and nutritional value of aquatic resources in rural livelihoods (Meusch et al, 2003). The assessment focused on Attapeu, one of the poorest provinces in Lao PDR.

While there is a need to improve rice production and cultivation, the expansion of rice cultivation into wetland and floodplain areas may affect the wild fishery. This cost has not been considered. Growing evidence now indicates that the widely diverse aquatic resources available in these wetland areas – including fish, snails, molluscs, crabs, frogs and plants harvested from floodplains, seasonal ponds and streams, as well as rice fields – provide the main source of animal protein in diets that otherwise lack protein. In Attapeu, harvesting aquatic resources is the main coping strategy for periods of rice deficit. There are no coping strategies for shortages of aquatic resources. Any loss of this wild resource will therefore have a significant impact on the nutritional status of local people, one which could not be replaced solely through increased rice production.

Meusch et al (2003, p19) note that, '[d]iversity is a key strategy for coping with the seasonal nature of rice production and other crops and varying availability of water resources'. Rice production and aquatic resource harvesting are necessary and inseparable components of livelihood strategies that need to be able to adapt to dramatic seasonal changes. Improved management of wild aquatic resources – rather than concentrating on rice production alone – has the potential to greatly improve nutritional status, and thus contribute to diverse, adaptable livelihood strategies. The kind of strategies that IUCN is promoting can make a significant contribution to both poverty reduction and conservation.

There are also important distributional issues to consider. Aquatic resources harvested from common property areas are particularly important to poor people, particularly those with less access to land and less capital to invest in land-based production. This includes the harvesting of non-fish aquatic resources, often by women and children, in backwater swamps, ponds and ditches. These resources are consumed within the household. Intensification of rice production requires the kind of resources and capital (land, labour and credit) that by definition are not available to poorer people. Rural development strategies that focus only on rice production, without considering the management of wild aquatic resources, are unlikely to benefit poorer people. Alternatively, building on the knowledge and capacities of local people to manage a wide range of wetland habitats has the potential to support a great diversity of aquatic animals and plants.

The importance to local livelihoods of aquatic resources and the habitats upon which they depend means that there are many opportunities for conservation to directly contribute to poverty reduction. As Meusch et al (2003, piii) argue:

> *strategies for rural development, food security and poverty alleviation... need to pay special attention to aquatic resource management to ensure the health and well-being of rural people. Integrated management of freshwater and wetland resources is necessary to meet the objectives of increased rice production whilst maintaining the viability and productivity of the aquatic resources upon which rural livelihoods depend.*

Implications of negotiated landscapes for protected areas

In cases where the protection of biodiversity is a top priority, i.e. where rare and highly susceptible species are involved, governments may decide to place part of a landscape under strict protection. Negotiations on a landscape level could help to resolve where the boundary falls and how people will be compensated. Livelihood functions would need to be provided elsewhere in the landscape as part of a compensation package.

Progressive contextualization

Dealing with questions of scale and multiple levels presents methodological difficulties. Boundaries are not always clear. The causes of local effects are often geographically remote or rooted in institutional factors. Further, the relevant physical boundaries will shift, depending on the issue being addressed. Short of methodological anarchy, how can the relevant boundaries be recognized in such circumstances?

Progressive contextualization is one useful approach. It has been described by the anthropologist and human ecologist Vayda (1983) and has since been used widely by political ecologists. Progressive contextualization involves 'focusing on significant human activities or people–environment interactions and then explaining these interactions by placing them within progressively wider or denser contexts' (Vayda, 1983, p265).

In other words, it starts with a problem or situation that needs to be explained and identifies contextual factors that seem to be relevant. As it explores these factors, new factors become identified and are explored in turn. There is no clear framework at the beginning to show what will be or will not be relevant. What is relevant emerges progressively.

The approach was originally proposed partly as a way to help human ecologists to address the persistent question of deciding 'the appropriate units of research' (Vayda, 1983, p266). Vayda quotes di Castri (1976, p245):

Human uses of the environment are not confined within ecosystems. Economic systems are specifically organised around the exchange of material, of energy, and even of people between ecosystems; they cut across ecosystems in order to take advantages of the complementarities and contrasts of different ecological zones.

As Vayda (1983) points out, the application of progressive contextualization requires avoiding assumptions (explicit or implicit) about the boundaries within which an issue should be addressed. An advantage of the approach is that it can help to deal with situations involving change and instability as well as 'phenomena that are, or are assumed to be, stable and persistent' (p277).

A further advantage of progressive contextualization is that it tends to avoid imposing standard solutions to locally distinct sets of problems. So what does this mean in practice? Shepherd (personal communication) argues that it is advisable to start with a landscape chosen with key stakeholders and then to broaden the focus if perceived problems cannot be solved. The point is that the boundaries are provisional and are expanded as appropriate when causes that need to be addressed cannot be addressed at the level originally selected. In this sense the expansion may be geographical (larger space) or into the wider institutional landscape.

Negotiated landscapes

The landscape concept is an entirely different way of looking at land use. Balancing land-use objectives over a wide scale is more useful than attempting to balance them at a site level. There are risks that the landscape concept can be used as a justification for centralized planning and an attempt to control the ways in which objectives are balanced. We are arguing for negotiated landscapes, not planned landscapes.[2] Particular views about how landscapes should be conserved (or if they should be conserved) should be negotiated with other stakeholders.

Whenever attempts are made to implement decentralized planning there is a tendency to revert to expert-driven land-use planning, perhaps with a little bit of community-level consultation thrown in for good measure. A number of well-intentioned conservation landscape (or ecosystem) approaches have inadvertently ended up reinforcing inequitable tenure and use rights and power relations, and exacerbating the insecurity of vulnerable rural livelihoods. Part of the problem is that even pluralistic planning approaches have their natural limits, which conservationists and other land-use experts, who are often only passingly acquainted with the social sciences, tend to ignore. The voices of the poor and dispossessed are rarely heard even at village-level participatory planning meetings.

One potential problem with the emphasis on pluralism and on multiple stakeholders underlying the landscape concept is that it can be a threat to community-managed resources. Asserting that a number of diverse stakeholders have an interest in management of a landscape can easily become an excuse for removing decision making away from a local community, often, in effect, putting resources back in control of interested parties who alienated benefits away from the communities in the first place – stakeholders such as commercial logging companies or forest departments. In this way landscape management and the associated multiple-stakeholder approach can be threats to the livelihoods of the poor. At the same time, 'recentralizing' undermines both the ethical and pragmatic arguments for community management. A negotiated approach to landscape management has to be based on a recognition of such threats and is not inconsistent with devolving authority to communities.

An approach that attempts to negotiate desirable landscape configurations will, in many occasions, fall short of both social and conservation expectations. Negotiation should not revolve around trying to determine an 'ideal' land-use configuration but should focus on the institutional and policy arrangements required to balance land-use trade-offs between social, environmental and economic interests, including the rights and interests of local communities. Where such trade-offs cannot be achieved, adequate and equitable compensatory mechanisms should be put in place. There is also a danger of placing too much reliance on using expert-driven mapping processes as planning tools, although they can be useful in supporting decisions.

While recognizing the potential for the landscape concept and its associated pluralism to be used in such a way that they threaten relatively powerless groups, we would argue that there is little real alternative and that the crucial need is to emphasize the importance of negotiation and to set in place equitable negotiating processes and fora. The case of the Ord River in northern Australia is a case where negotiations between indigenous people and other interests have lead to what is effectively a 'landscape agreement' (in this case formally called an Indigenous

Land Use Agreement) that involves trade-offs between different types of land use, including recognition of the cultural rights of Aboriginal people (see Box 4.4). Significantly, the Aboriginal people were prepared to trade some parts of their traditional 'country' to water users in exchange for rights to jointly manage areas of cultural importance as conservation areas.

Box 4.4 The Ord River Indigenous Land Use Agreement

The Ord catchment is a part of the traditional country belonging to Miriuwung, Gajerrong and Kija peoples and is a transboundary catchment in northern Australia that spans the West Australia–Northern Territory border. It covers about 46,100km² and encompasses multiple values ranging from high conservation priorities with three Ramsar sites to sustaining traditional livelihoods of local indigenous peoples. Two dams on the Ord mainstream capture water for, among other things, the irrigation of 15,000 hectares and the creation of hydropower for diamond mining in the south of the catchment. Construction of these dams began in 1969 and the Ord Main Dam was opened in 1973. The hydrological transformation of the Ord occurred without consideration of the impacts on the local indigenous people dispossessed by the damming of the river, exacerbating the severe impacts of the first stage of irrigation development. These impacts include social and economic marginalization (Kimberley Land Council, 2004).

Through recent native title negotiations, this omission is being remedied with an US$54 million compensation package for both past acts and the surrendering of native title to facilitate further irrigation expansion in the Ord. Native title consists of those rights and interests of Aboriginal and Torres Strait Islander people in land and water, according to their traditional laws and customs, which are recognized under Australian law. After ten years of litigation failed to bring about resolution between disputing parties, negotiations began in 2003 between Miriuwung and Gajerrong traditional owners (represented by the Kimberley Land Council) and the West Australian government. Negotiations were supported financially by the state. This process culminated in a negotiated agreement signed by the state, traditional owners and private interests. The Ord Final Agreement (Government of Western Australia, 2005) is the name of this Indigenous Land Use Agreement formed through these negotiations and it stipulates a range of governance changes in the Ord. One important change is the setting up of six conservation reserves that are to be jointly managed by traditional owner representatives for an area and the Department of Environment and Conservation, the government body with statutory responsibility for management of conservation areas.

The renegotiated landscape of the Ord attempts to provide opportunities for traditional owners to continue – and in some instances reconnect with – their 'caring for country', a concept that refers to indigenous Australians being able to access important sites for cultural practices and managing the complex environmental interactions that sustain them. Access to country is seen as an important cultural right by the indigenous people in the area. As one Miriuwung traditional owner pointed out, the importance of the 'right to access my country' was the reason why her people had campaigned for so long to get recognition of native title rights. This principle is included in management of the new conservation areas that are designed to provide for conservation, recreation and tourism, while protecting the environmental and cultural heritage of the region. The negotiated agreement also allocates indigenous peoples parcels of community purpose land within the Ord catchment at Yardungarrl and at East Kununurra. Community purpose land is intended to provide security to the traditional owners adversely affected by the earlier developments. In addition, the final package consists of a range of initiatives that focus on improving the capacity of indigenous people to engage in the local economy and benefit from any future development. Through surrendering native title to some country, indigenous people were able to secure compensation as well as support for participation in future development opportunities.

The recent governance transformations dramatically reconfigure elements of social, economic, environmental and cultural interactions in the Ord. The promise of this 'living document' (Tehan et al, 2006) lies in its implementation; the negotiation process began essential dispute processing that arose from unjust natural resource management acts by a settling state. What remains to be seen is whether the perception of the available opportunities for indigenous people to effectively participate in this new framework carries through to a meaningful reality.

Source: Provided by Jess McLean, University of Sydney

Some conservationists may be concerned that such a 'negotiated' landscape concept, driven by enabling institutional and policy interventions (or by dismantling institutional and policy constraints) that contribute to poverty reduction, will make it even more difficult to ensure that biologically important parts of the landscape are secured for conservation. More fundamentally, they may feel that it will be nearly impossible to gazette new protected areas. We argue the reverse on two counts:

- Historically, landscape configuration has been shaped much more by policy and institutional interventions than through considered and deliberate large-scale planning. There is nothing to suggest that conditions have changed, although market forces may play a more significant role. By working through proven drivers of landscape change conservationists stand a much better chance of securing outcomes that are good for conservation.
- A 'negotiated' landscape concept does not preclude gazetting new protected areas or mean that local rights and values are automatically given precedence over global (or national) public values. What it does is provide a process whereby enabling institutional and policy arrangements can be put in place to ensure that poor communities are not disadvantaged and/or are adequately and fairly compensated. Properly negotiated gazetting of protected areas that pays attention to institutional and policy support systems is more likely to minimize conflict and secure long-term conservation success.

Conservation and development literature places increasing emphasis on pluralism. In forest conservation, for example, there is a clear recognition that many different stakeholders have an interest in forest management and policy and that long-term management decisions and policy need to take account of at least major stakeholders' interests (see for example Anderson et al, 1998; Wollenberg et al, 2001b).[3]

The rationale for including multiple stakeholders in resource management decisions has a pragmatic aspect (including people who carry out natural resource management in decision making increases the likelihood that they will modify their practices in conformity with stakeholder agreements) as well as an ethical one (including people who will be affected by forest management decisions will make it more likely that decisions will reflect their needs and interests).

It is important to remember that many different types of specific interests can exist within a community and even within the category 'poor'. People are poor or subject to the risk of becoming poor for different reasons, depending on such factors as which resource they depend on for livelihoods. Within a single rural community, some people may rely on fishing, others on horticulture. Resource management decisions may affect them differently. Women are often affected differently than men, particularly because of gender-based labour differences. Even the category 'women' often (even usually) may need to be differentiated. For equity, stakeholder negotiations must recognize this diversity and it is fundamental to poverty reduction that different patterns of poverty be recognized and dealt with.

While the landscape concept is very important and pluralism is an essential part of the approach, there are risks involved in pluralist approaches. One is that the stakeholders most likely to negotiate effectively are those with power and influence, precisely those who probably already dominate decision making. Those least likely to achieve their desired outcomes will tend to be the poor and politically marginalized – people who are already relatively disempowered. Pluralism in forest policy may inadvertently reinforce the interests of powerful commercial interests, conservation groups or forest departments at the expense of forest-dependent rural communities.

A number of authors have recognized the need to structure pluralist stakeholder negotiations in order to recognize the needs of the less powerful (Wollenberg et al, 2001a). Colfer et al (1999) explore ways to assess the extent to which different interests in forest management should be given relatively more or less attention. The extent of forest dependency is one factor that justifies paying particular attention to particular groups of stakeholders.

The assumption behind negotiated landscapes is that the power to make decisions is meaningfully devolved to participants. This does not mean that all participants will achieve their objectives, but that they will have a meaningful role in negotiating outcomes and making decisions. In this context, participation in stakeholder fora must involve more than token forms of negotiation such as consultation (see Arnstein, 1969, for a typology of different types of participation ranging from tokenism to genuine citizen power).

The need for pluralist approaches to landscape negotiations is one thing, carrying out such negotiations is another. The goal is to establish and facilitate negotiation processes that create a more or less level playing field and assist parties to focus on their real objectives rather than on peripheral issues.

Negotiation and level playing fields

We argue that win–win solutions for both conservation and development are not always – or not often – likely. Nevertheless, negotiation and trade-offs do occur and are necessary and there are often opportunities for 'win-more–lose-less' outcomes. There is a need to think of objectives and trade-offs in a way that minimizes conflict (or at least eliminates unnecessary conflict), allows negotiation to focus on essentials and allows for innovative approaches.

Some important insights are contained in the literature on conflict management. One important idea from conflict management theory is that parties in negotiations should not 'argue over positions' (Fisher and Ury, 1981). Fisher and Ury argue that it is essential to focus on interests, not positions.

An example of this in conservation would be a debate about whether people should be allowed to take domestic livestock into a protected area. If parties argued from positions, the park authorities would insist that domestic animals be entirely banned from protected areas and livestock owners would insist that they be allowed to take livestock into the protected area whenever it suited them. This would lead to an impasse where no resolution was likely. If, however, interests are considered rather than positions, it might become clear that the park authorities' main concern is winter grazing for wild herbivores being affected by domestic livestock.[4] Alternatively, the livestock owners may only want access to the grazing areas in the park at the beginning of summer when planting activities outside the park leave little time to manage their herds, whereas lightly supervised grazing in the park requires little labour. In such a situation there will be little direct conflict between the underlying interests of the two parties and compromise should be possible. It is only if either party takes an unyielding position that a negotiated solution would be impossible. In other words, negotiation works best if it focuses on interests and outcomes rather than preordained positions.

In cases such as this, the conflict between stakeholders can appear to be intractable, but the essential interests may be relatively easy to accommodate. This does not mean that intractable conflicts do not occur. Win–lose outcomes are sometimes inevitable. As Warner (2001) argues, however, consensus solutions are better than compromise solutions if they are possible.

We argue that the potential for meeting the interests of different stakeholders is increased if negotiations operate beyond the level of specific sites. In addition to thinking about how the content of negotiations can be better framed in order to avoid unnecessary conflict, it is also important to think about the process of negotiations and how it can be structured to give all stakeholders a fair opportunity to argue their interests.

When different stakeholders negotiate over resources and land use, it is common for some groups to be disadvantaged (this is often true of poor people in rural communities). There are a number of reasons for this:

• Negotiations cost time and money, especially when they involve large commercial interests or government bureaucracies. Some negotiations continue for months or even years and people from rural communities (especially poor people) cannot afford to commit the large amount of time required, losing income while they do so. They frequently cannot afford to pay for professional support (such as lawyers). Some stakeholders simply have more 'staying power' during protracted negotiations or court processes.
• Negotiations often take place in an atmosphere dominated by technical language or legal concepts inaccessible to the poor and to non-specialists.
• Where stakeholders come from different subgroups within a community, wealthy local people are more likely to have good working relationships with and influence on government agents and decision makers.
• The parameters for decision making are often set in advance by non-local actors. For example, government policies may limit the room for negotiation and rule out meaningful solutions.
• Community participation is often in the form of attendance by community representatives, sometimes appointed in some way by the community and sometimes selected or appointed by outsiders. Expectations of the role of representatives, even when they are regarded as legitimate by a community, may vary. For example, outsiders may see them as having a mandate to reach agreement on behalf of a community, whereas community members may view them as mere intermediaries.

In this context of often highly skewed opportunities for satisfactorily negotiated outcomes for many poor or disempowered groups, creating a more level playing field for landscape-level negotiations is crucial. As Wollenberg et al (2001a) point out, this requires a strategy to ensure that the needs of the 'less powerful' are met. This is obviously directly relevant for conservation that aims to meet the needs of the poor. Wollenberg et al (2001a, p218) propose the following:

> ... *accommodation that genuinely reflects the interests of disadvantaged groups is most likely to occur where a combination of state and civil society governance institutions provide for 1) the discovery and transformation of values and interests through mutual leaning among interest groups, 2) iterative cycles of*

bounded conflict and negotiation, 3) public, transparent decision-making, 4) checks and balances in decision-making among groups, and 5) explicit support for disadvantaged interest groups.

In addition to the strategy suggested by Wollenberg et al, several other elements can help ensure equity in negotiations over landscapes. Perhaps more importantly, there should be a neutral facilitator for negotiations. This may not always be possible, but it is essential to ensure that all parties trust the facilitator to be fair. The facilitator and convenor (if these are two separate individuals) should not be seen as having strong vested interests in particular outcomes.

It is often worth having an outsider, with no connections to other stakeholders, to act as an advocate or supporter, especially to advise on procedures that guide stakeholders through arcane legal or administrative processes or to act as a mediator or 'honest broker'. This task can sometimes be carried out by umbrella groups such as federations of users' organizations. Members of such federations often have experience in similar issues.

Another practical way to assist disempowered groups in negotiations is to help them in preparing or presenting their case, perhaps by supporting participatory appraisal or providing training in negotiating skills (Warner, 2001).

Scheduling the negotiation process so that it consists of a series of shorter meetings with intervals to reflect can be a useful way to spread the costs of protracted negotiations and can enable people to discuss and assimilate the significance of proposals. This is particularly important where community representatives need time to obtain a clear mandate from the community.

Where groups or communities are represented by individuals in negotiations, it is essential that these representatives either operate with a clear mandate as to what they can or cannot accept in negotiations, or that there is a mechanism for communities to accept or reject decisions. The question of representation is difficult, and mechanisms to ensure the legitimacy of representatives are essential (Wollenberg and McDougall, personal communication). Culturally sensitive processes of representation are extremely important; the concept of elected or appointed representatives making decisions on behalf of a group is not present in many cultures. Issues of representation are particularly important when negotiations occur at national or even global levels but also apply to landscape-level negotiations.

Conclusions

This chapter has explored some important elements of the conceptual basis for an approach to linking conservation and poverty reduction:

• The causes of both conservation and poverty problems are often distant from sites where their effects are felt. It is important to address these remote causes.

- Since causes may be geographically or institutionally remote, it is important to think of multiple geographical scales and multiple institutional levels.
- Identifying potential connections between conservation and poverty reduction/livelihoods is often unrealistic at a site level and makes more sense at a landscape level. A landscape concept encompasses a broader range of opportunities for trade-offs.
- The landscape concept is about negotiated outcomes, not centralized planning.
- In order to reduce poverty and increase livelihood benefits from negotiations it is essential to develop mechanisms that empower the poor in negotiations.
- Recognizing the heterogeneity within communities is essential in order to deal with the variety of people and the variety of effects of poverty.

Chapter 5 looks at some ways in which an approach based on these concepts can be put into practice.

Notes

1 The following discussion of the landscape concept draws heavily on Maginnis et al (2004).
2 The landscape perspective implies a decentralized approach to land-use decision making, in which decisions are devolved to as local a level as is practical, including very often the community level. This does not mean that there is no centralized role in setting standards or broad objectives for natural resource and land management. The balance between centralized planning and negotiated landscapes is further discussed in Chapter 5.
3 Who are legitimate stakeholders? The World Commission on Dams (WCD, 2000) proposes a rights-and-risks approach that is useful in defining which stakeholders' interests should be considered. The approach identifies people who are at risk from an intervention or change and sees them as having rights as stakeholders.
4 One of the difficulties in negotiating objectives for land use is precisely that many people see their positions as being based on absolute values and their objectives as consequently non-negotiable. This applies to views about the absolute value of wilderness, to the primacy of scientific management or to various competing claims about rights to resources. Genuine negotiation to some extent depends on acceptance that objectives and rights are always claims subject to negotiation.

Structures, Institutions and Rights

Introduction

Chapter 4 discussed using the landscape concept as a way of linking conservation and poverty reduction by working at multiple physical scales. This chapter looks at the importance of addressing issues at various institutional levels and at the importance of institutions as opportunities and constraints.

The World Bank defines poverty in terms of lack of assets, powerlessness and vulnerability (see Chapter 2). As that definition acknowledges, there are serious limitations in focusing too much on a lack of assets. Rural people frequently have ready access to potentially valuable livelihood assets. The problem is in converting them into positive outcomes in livelihoods terms. Many kinds of constraints, including those the World Bank includes under the heading of powerlessness, affect the capability of people to use their assets. In many protected areas, for example, the poverty of resident or nearby peoples is not the result of an absence of assets or resources, but the fact that these assets cannot be legally collected or sold.

Thus, poverty is not just a lack of assets, or a site-specific problem, but is subject to wider factors, such as a lack of legal access to resources, inadequate marketing systems and other limitations, including policy constraints. Interestingly, conservation is also often seen in terms of assets (such as protected areas) and interventions are often site-specific.

In Lao PDR, the IUCN NTFP Project (Case Study 3) aimed to contribute to conservation by providing incentives for people to conserve forest resources. Improved production and marketing of NTFPs were seen as ways to generate income that would provide such incentives. As the project explored the linkages between conservation and income generation, however, the emphasis shifted from 'conservation through incentives' to 'conservation by removing constraints'. While the constraints were originally seen as barriers to conservation, it became apparent that they were also constraints to poverty reduction. Removing the constraints in the Lao case was an example of establishing 'transforming processes' in terms of the DFID livelihoods framework, and in that case the processes were new institutional arrangements (agreed ways of doing things).

It is not that conservation cannot work by providing incentives or that incentives for conservation cannot contribute to poverty reduction. Clearly they can. Initiatives such as carbon transfers and payments for environmental services may, in some cases, be useful and legitimate ways of addressing both poverty and conservation concerns. The use of incentives is only one of a number of tools, however, and one that cannot be applied everywhere.

Linking poverty reduction and conservation by removing constraints, or by supporting transforming structures and processes, implies that one of the most useful interventions for outsiders is providing facilitation for communities and assisting them to assess their opportunities and plan coordinated action. In Pred Nai (Case Study 1), outside intervention supported networking activities (institution building) and provided technical support for mangrove management planning.

Chapter 1 noted the number of often contradictory assertions about the causal relationships between elements such as poverty, conservation and environmental degradation. None of these propositions is universally true; causes are complex and specific to situations. They are also affected by a variety of institutional arrangements that mediate between causes and effects. This chapter explores the ways in which institutional arrangements can be modified to link conservation and poverty reduction.

Brown (2003) argues that one of the key reasons why attempts to integrate conservation and development have so often been unsuccessful is the frequent misfit between institutions and 'the ecosystems they seek to manage' (p479). 'There is the problem of fit – both between the institutions involved in integrating conservation and development (in terms of their objectives, interests and worldviews), and their respective scales of operations' (Brown, 2003, p480). Brown's argument is a reminder that it is not only necessary to have institutions to regulate resource use, but that these institutions must include the relevant actors and be appropriate to the ecosystem resource.

Community institutions

In the past much of the emphasis in ICDPs was on developing community institutions and organizations to manage natural resources. Although this is obviously important, in many cases new institutions were developed when existing institutions were capable of managing resources. In many cases they already did manage resources. An extensive body of literature exists on indigenous or local systems of natural resource management (especially forests and water resources) and on institutions for managing common property resources (see for example Uphoff, 1986, 1992; Fisher, 1989, 1994; Ostrom, 1990; Murphree, 1993).

Common property is an example of the way in which appropriate institutional arrangements can shape resource use. The theory of 'the tragedy of the commons' (Hardin, 1968) suggested that resources without clear ownership would be degraded because individuals would have no incentive to reduce their level of resource use if other people continued their use at unsustainable levels. Everyone would attempt to maximize use in the short term even when they could see long-term availability declining. This implied that management of resources in a commons is inevitably unsustainable, an example of an over-generalized causal proposition. Hardin mistakenly ignored the fact that people do not act solely as individuals, but that they can develop agreements that regulate resource use. In other words, they build institutions. The common-property literature shows that, in many cases, communities have developed functioning institutions that regulate resource use. It also attempts to identify the types of factors that lead to effective institutions.

This is not to say that local institutions are always effective. There are many cases of degraded resources that make this clear. Institutions may be ineffective either because the agreed rules of behaviour that they incorporate do not lead to the desired effects on ecosystems (for example, they allow removal of too many reproducing fish), or because they are not respected or enforced. Sometimes institutions do not include people with the capacity to affect resource management. For example, institutional arrangements for management of a particular fish pond may involve people from one village but exclude people living on the other side of the pond. In Brown's (2003) terms, there is a mismatch between the institutional arrangements for making decisions about resource use and the resource to be managed.

Institutions for resource management must be able to deal with heterogeneous interests, especially equity and gender. Experiences in community-based resource management consistently show that community-level institutions and organizations tend to be dominated by powerful individuals and groups. This has major implications for institutions linking poverty reduction and conservation. In a study of the impacts of community forestry in Nepal, Malla (2000) shows that the poor often end up with reduced access to forest resources after community forests are created. This is partly because user groups are dominated by relatively wealthy people who have different needs than poor people. The rules governing access reflect their interests and not those of the poor. Ironically, rules guaranteeing equal access to forest products may disadvantage the poor. Prior to the handover of forests to communities the wealthy tended to get much of their fuelwood from private land, while the poor obtained most of theirs from forests.

Rules that specify a set amount per household have little impact on wealthy households, but may actually mean that poor households get less fuelwood than before.

In the case of community forestry in Nepal, there have been positive conservation outcomes but the approach has failed to adequately address the needs of the poor. Reducing poverty would require facilitation of institution-building processes. This would include paying careful attention to specific groups, including the poor and women (whose workloads may be significantly affected by changes in rules and regulations, but who tend to be greatly under-represented in decision-making processes).[1] Historically, extension support has tended to come from government staff, but NGOs and users networks are increasingly playing the facilitator role.

Institutional arrangements for tenure and access

One of the main themes in community-based natural resource management is the importance of establishing rights to resources. The dominant view among resource management theorists and practitioners is that people are most likely to become involved in sustainable management when they have clear rights to resources. Clearly defined rights provide an incentive for active participation and sustainable use because they guarantee access to resources. In fact, many advocates of community-based natural resource management see resource tenure, in the form of full legal ownership, as essential in providing benefits from natural resources to local people. However, cases such as Pred Nai, where the community has no legal tenure, certainly call into question the idea that clear tenure is always a prerequisite for community-based conservation action. Fisher (1995) argues that confidence about future access, whether based on formal tenure or not, is more crucial than formal title. In fact, legal rights are not always enforced and may even be ignored by government agencies, while oral agreements may be sufficient if there is a history of their being honoured (Fisher, 1995). Both formal and informal institutions may be effective in different circumstances (for a discussion of tenure, see Box 5.1).

Although it is clear that people will sometimes 'participate' without full legal tenure, rights are often the key to achieving levels of poverty reduction through natural resource use. This is clear from Shinyanga (Case Study 2) and ACOFOP (Case Study 5). Some economists, notably de Soto (2000) have argued that clear and formal systems of property rights are essential for poverty reduction and that the presence of such formal systems is the key to entrepreneurship and economic growth. De Soto places stress on private property rights. It is important to realize, however, that privatizing 'communal' resources often disadvantages the poor who often fail to gain private shares and may lose access to natural resources altogether.

In any case, presuming rights are widely distributed and enforceable, clear

Box 5.1 Tenure, natural resources and poverty

Security of tenure is a critical yet often under-acknowledged component in determining how rural people can improve their livelihoods and reduce poverty. Tenure encompasses the rights of secure, long-term access to land and resources, their benefits and the responsibilities related to these rights.

Leach et al (1999) emphasize 'environmental entitlements', which are 'alternative sets of utilities [benefits] derived from environmental goods and services over which social actors have legitimate effective command and which are instrumental in achieving well-being' (p233) They link these 'entitlements' to 'endowments', which they define as 'the rights and resources that social actors have. For example, land, labour, skills and so on' (p233). An understanding of endowments is important since the level of resource richness in a given community clearly affects the resource and demand ratios involved.

As Barrow and Murphree (2001) discuss, these terms have important dimensions:

- These rights are rarely, if ever, absolute, but the longer their sanctioned duration, the stronger their tenure will be. Their strengths are determined by their time frames and the conditions attached. The fewer the conditions attached to them, the stronger their ownership will be. As Alchian says, the strength of ownership 'can be defined by the extent to which the owner's decision to use the resource actually determines its use' (Alchian, 1987, p1031).
- These rights have a number of derivations. They can be conferred by the state, in their strong form as de jure rights or in weaker versions as de facto rights. They can arise from customary law derived from the norms and practices of long established non-state cultures and social groupings, or they can be the results of particular configurations of power in specific contexts of social interaction. The legitimacy of these derivations is dynamic and frequently contested. In many countries, conflicts between statutory and customary law are endemic, creating a dissonance in resource claims and usage (Okoth-Owiro, 1988).
- Rights require regimes of authority, from small social units (such as a household or partnership) to the state. The scale is influenced by the nature of the resource over which rights are exercised. Generally, resources are classified in a four-fold typology of state property, private property, common property and open-access resources. This typology, developed in common property theory, is analytically useful but can be misleading when the resource and the regime are combined. 'Open access' resources do not constitute a regime; their defining characteristic is in fact the absence of a regime. 'Common property' resources, defined as 'a class of resources for which exclusion is difficult and joint use involves subtractability' (Berkes, 1989, p7), are not necessarily managed by a communal regime. They are often managed by a state regime, the management of the water of a large catchment area being a good example. 'Private property' is not necessarily individual property; it may be corporate property managed by a corporate, private regime.
- Rights confer authority as well as responsibility, and these need to be functionally linked. When they are de-linked and assigned to different institutional actors, both are eroded. Authority without responsibility becomes meaningless or obstructive; responsibility without authority lacks the necessary instrumental and motivational components for its efficient exercise.

and reasonably secure tenure obviously has implications for the poor. Supporting community-based conservation with enforceable rights is essentially a form of empowerment.

It is important to note that while the value of secure access rights has an effect at the local level, the institutional change that supports it generally comes from policies or laws enacted at a state or national level. Addressing poverty reduction and conservation needs to work both at the local level (facilitating equitable decision making and distribution of benefits within a community) and at wider policy levels (using policy processes to provide supportive institutional mechanisms). Local action is supported by wider institutions.

Institutions at the landscape level

Chapter 4 outlined the idea that negotiated landscapes presented challenges resulting from the need to create equal opportunities in the negotiation process among stakeholders and the tension between decentralized decision making and centralized planning and coordination. As Brown (2003) points out, it is difficult to design an institution 'that can accommodate different interests and includes diverse individuals' (p485). This is true at the community level. It is even more important at landscape scales and in cases where actors and stakeholders come from distant locations and institutions.

The central challenge at the landscape level is to establish institutional arrangements that can enable meaningful negotiations between individual and institutional stakeholders with diverse and competing interests and different levels of power.

Devolution and decentralization

The landscape perspective requires a decentralized approach to land use, where decisions are made at as local a level as is practical, often the community level. Devolution of decision making rarely occurs in practice, however. Genuinely devolved and negotiated decision making is essential for empowering people to manage resources. This does not mean that there is no role for central authorities in setting standards or broad objectives for natural resource and land management. The problem is how to do this without undermining local decision making and effectively recentralizing control.

The move towards devolution and decentralization of government and administration has been a major international trend in governance in recent years. This has been evident in many fields, including resource management. Often the emphasis has been on devolution and management to communities and local natural resource users rather than to local- and district-level governments. This section focuses on the process of devolution and decentralization to the community level rather than to local government. It is clear that the trend toward devolution is often more rhetoric than reality, at least in the sense that power and authority are not always devolved.

Although the terminology is not always consistent, it is useful to differentiate between devolution and decentralization. Fisher (1999) defines decentralization as 'the relocation of administrative functions away from a central location' and devolution as 'the relocation of power away from a central location' (p3). Other authors refer to decentralization of power as 'political decentralization' (see, for example, Tacconi, 2006).

There is much more evidence of decentralization of administrative functions (and responsibility) away from centrally located agencies than of devolution of power to make and implement decisions. Perhaps one of the major reasons for this is that devolution and decentralization have often been driven by crises – particularly financial crises – that have caused governments to offload financial responsibility for activities such as resource management.

Tension often exists between genuine devolved decision making and government's and government agencies' need to feel that they are able to monitor trends and set overall objectives. If power is genuinely devolved, governments cannot predict what the outcomes of decisions will be. In some cases, governments set guidelines and regulations that severely limit local decision making. For example, community forestry rules and regulations may restrict the type of products allowed to be collected and distributed from a forest (and perhaps include only dry fuelwood). If this is the case, local people can make decisions only about the process of collection and distribution, not about ways to manage the forest for sustainable production of fuelwood. This is hardly empowerment. It is also unlikely to achieve the level of participation needed to promote sustainable practices or to meet the needs of the poor.

The question is whether there is an alternative approach that substantially empowers local resource users and also meets the needs of the government for safeguards against excessive or unsustainable use of resources. There is a need to make decision makers responsible for their decisions, without the constraint of too many detailed guidelines. Ribot (2002) has argued that this can be achieved by providing limited guidelines about broad outputs along with a minimum list of what cannot be done, rather than a long list prescribing what must be done. He refers to this as a 'minimum standards approach'.

If sound local decision making is to be possible, local institutions must be developed and strengthened. While they need to be accountable upwards (in such matters as safeguards for environmental standards), they also need to be accountable downwards, to the people they represent. Ribot (2002) argues that to be effective in natural resource management, local institutions must be accountable downwards and genuinely representative: 'Decentralization requires both *power transfers* and *accountable representation*' (p6, emphasis original).

This has obvious importance in conservation involving poverty reduction;

true representation requires that different stakeholders and groups within a local population (including the poor) have their views represented and seriously considered. Ribot points out that responsiveness to the poor is a relatively rare outcome of decentralization. Tacconi (2006) argues that, in countries with 'relatively poor governance systems', characterized by 'weak representative decision-making processes [in which] local elites and vested interest groups can often manipulate the institutions and opportunities created by decentralization for their own benefit' (p341), 'democratic decentralization' will be difficult to implement. Developing institutions that represent the poor is difficult, especially because poverty is not a priority of local elites, but it is an essential step.[2]

The wider institutional landscape

Non-timber forest products in India

In India, joint forest management (JFM) aims to promote afforestation through cooperation between communities and various state forest departments. One important aspect of JFM is generating income from the collection and sale of NTFPs. An analysis by Sarin (1998) shows that institutional factors impose limitations on poor people's capacity to earn income:

- Monopoly rights for collecting and marketing certain products were vested in specific agencies or private companies. For example, rights to 29 NTFPs in Orissa were vested in one private company (as of 1998). The people who collect the products 'invariably among the poorest members of their communities and predominantly women, continue[d] to receive only wages for their labour, often at abysmally low rates for the time and effort required for collection' (p24).
- In Gujarat, *adivasi* (tribal) processors had to obtain licences for every step of their activities (buying raw material, transporting and selling). They paid far more than commercial companies did for the same products and services.

The important point from Sarin's study is that the barrier to income generation and poverty reduction is not simply limited availability of resources, lack of access to resources or a lack of markets for NTFPs, but can also be in the form of policies and regulations. These limit the share of benefits and, in practice, disproportionately affect the ability of the poor to earn income from resources. This is an institutional problem involving policies; addressing poverty would involve a policy change to remove the institutional constraints.

What is unsettling about Sarin's study is the suggestion that the existing policy serves vested interests. Changing policies often requires challenging these powerful groups. Natural resource management is essentially about competing interests.[3]

Institutional change and power

Institutions consist of policies, laws, markets and other rules and arrangements. They are formed and applied by people, sometimes individuals, sometimes through organizations. Changing institutions often involves transforming individual people, relationships and institutional actors. Often a change in attitude is required before institutional arrangements can become effective.

Efforts at institutional change to support activities such as CBNRM or collaborative management of protected areas have often focused on developing staff capacity through training in knowledge and skills. They have sometimes focused more explicitly on changing elitist and anti-people attitudes. Where successes have been reported in changing attitudes, training has usually included participatory exercises. These allow government staff and other trainees to develop a greater awareness of the legitimate points of view of rural people. Courses based on traditional lecturing methods have not generally been successful in changing attitudes.[4]

Even where efforts are made to stimulate attitudinal change through participatory and experiential training, trainees often return to work situations that do not support new attitudes or provide opportunities to apply them in practice. Without a supporting institutional environment, old attitudes and ways of thinking tend to reassert themselves. Little if any evidence exists to show that training alone leads to long-term change in attitudes or that new attitudes lead to changed working styles. The most promising approach seems to be a combination of short periods of field-based training and initiatives to implement new approaches.

The difficulty in changing the way conservation and natural resource management agencies relate to rural people is that the issues are not merely knowledge, skills and attitudes, but power and vested interests. Perhaps the biggest barrier in promoting attitudinal change is that negative attitudes to rural people and a reluctance to adopt more people-friendly approaches tend to be associated with personal interests. Because of professional pride and concerns over prestige, power and even direct financial interests, resource managers often feel threatened by sharing power. Attitudes and personal interests tend to be mutually reinforcing.

Poverty is an outcome of contested resources and contested objectives. Power is essentially relative: some people are poor and powerless because others are rich and powerful. Empowering people to negotiate with authorities over natural resource management is probably as important as changing attitudes. It is important to develop mechanisms or institutions that empower people. This includes supporting the development of community and user networks, alliances and partnerships.

ACOFOP (Case Study 5) illustrates the role of outsiders in supporting this type of process. In Pred Nai (Case Study 1), the villagers themselves found that linking with other villages to form a network of people concerned with mangrove management was an effective way to increase their influence. They also linked with some NGOs and university academics who were able to assist them with specific tasks.

In Nepal, the Federation of Community Forest Users of Nepal (FECOFUN) was formed to assist different community forest user groups in working together.

Box 5.2 A regional network in Central America

The *Asociación Co-ordinadora Indígena y Campesina de Agroforestería Comunitária de Centroamerica* (CICIAFOC), or Central American Coordination Association for Indigenous and Peasant Community Agroforestry, was established in 1994 to help organize farmers to learn from each other and share experiences in small-scale agriculture and forestry production within Central America. It is a network of 65 indigenous and peasant farmer organizations such as community cooperatives, and member farms are vetted to ensure that they are community-run and owned.

CICIAFOC has become one of the most effective regional coordination bodies that represent the rights and interests of small-scale, often poor, farmers. The fact that it is a self-mobilized initiative that has allowed small farmers and farmer associations to represent their own interest, in their own words, gives it an authority that other champions of community forestry do not possess. It is more difficult for governments to ignore what CICIAFOC says.

Its mission recognizes that addressing issues of equity and power is fundamental to improving the lot of their members and safeguarding the environment. The equity issues it deals with range from the household level – such as women's access to and rights over natural resources – to the international (the need for local communities to receive fair compensation for the delivery of global public goods).

Despite CICIAFOC's impressive track record, challenges remain. A recent review of community forest networks indicated that building capacity among its membership organizations was a primary need (Colchester et al, 2003). The CICIAFOC experience highlights a number of key lessons for poverty reduction and conservation:

- Local communities appear to have less difficulty in realizing what sustainable development means in practice than do many international development and conservation organizations. They see the way to economic improvement as tied inextricably to good stewardship of the environment. What they advocate and what they do is a tacit rejection of 'develop now, protect later'.
- Although better technical advice on agriculture production is important, real change requires addressing issues of power and equity.
- In order to bring about change, action is needed at multiple scales and multiple institutional and policy levels. CICIAFOC has interventions at the level of farms, concessions, landscapes and region (Mesoamerican Biological Corridor). It also has political and institutional activities from the community-based organization level up to regional development and environmental processes.

FECOFUN gradually took on more of an advocacy role. It supported community interests generally, helping them resist the tendency of the forest department to attempt to limit community rights and control user groups. FECOFUN has been accused of being politicized; this is hardly surprising given that controlling forest resources is about power and the forest department certainly feels threatened by the increasing influence of FECOFUN.

Another example of a federation that contributes to empowerment of the poor, this time on a regional level, is CICIAFOC[5] in Central America (see Box 5.2).

Alliances such as CICIAFOC are largely peoples' initiatives. Large groups are able to speak with a louder voice than individuals. In general, advocates of poverty reduction in conservation need to be careful not to do too much when promoting initiatives such as these. It is better to allow them to rise from the efforts of local people. A more useful role is to support them by creating space for debate and information-sharing and provide access to advice and assistance where requested.

Economic institutions and instruments

Poverty reduction and conservation can be achieved through institutional change at a number of levels; they can also be supported by changing economic institutions. Economic theorists commonly believe that conservation problems occur because of market and policy failure and that corrections to markets and policies provide solutions. This is based on an assumption that individuals make rational decisions on the basis of market information. The field of institutional economics[6] emphasizes the fact that individual economic behaviour is constrained by shared rules, that markets are often constrained by institutions and – a point that is often ignored – that markets are themselves institutions. The implication of this is that market-based economic 'instruments' can be applied in such a way as to influence outcomes in desired directions.

Economists have proposed a number of market and non-market instruments for financing conservation, many of which have the potential to contribute to poverty reduction. (Such economic instruments are, of course, institutional arrangements.) Some examples of market-based instruments are markets for carbon sequestration and for watershed services. Market-based instruments such as payment for environmental services (PES) are designed to generate funds from users of resources (such as companies that generate carbon or downstream users of water) to be transferred as payments to people who provide environmental services, such as planting trees to trap carbon, or people who protect watersheds.

In a careful examination of the practicalities of PES, Wunder (2005) looks specifically at 'pro-poor PES'. He argues that there are structural constraints to 'pro-poor PES'. The first of these is that 'the "poorest of the poor" often do not own or control any land, thus directly ruling them out as PES service providers' (p17). He goes on to point out that the poor often have only informal tenure. Another structural 'constraint is the high transaction costs of dealing with many smallholders... compared to only a few big landowners' (Wunder, 2005, p22). Pagiola et al (2004), reviewing experiences from Latin America, argue that there is little conclusive evidence related to connections between PES and poverty. They stress that synergies are possible if programmes are well-designed and depending on local conditions.

Carbon sequestration schemes suffer from similar constraints. There is an additional problem: the risk that agreements between large companies and governments will lock forests up and lead to increased restrictions on local use, thus potentially exacerbating rather than reducing poverty.

In general, there are few, if any, examples of the benefits of these mechanisms actually reaching the poor. They may have the potential to contribute to poverty reduction, but they need to be modified so that they can be focused on the poor. As with many of the institutions discussed above, they are not intrinsically aimed at benefiting the poor.

National poverty reduction planning processes

Poverty reduction strategy papers (PRSPs) also have the potential to improve interactions between conservation and poverty reduction, although they have had limited success in this respect. There are two main reasons for this:

1   Conservationists have not systematically collected the type of data on the economic value of renewable natural resources to the poor that national economic planners find convincing or compelling.
2   Conservation and sustainable natural resource management have not been mainstreamed in poverty reduction strategies. Not only have conservation activities not generally been included in economic planning for poverty reduction but conservation agencies (including government departments with conservation roles) have generally treated poverty reduction as being outside their essential area of responsibility.

There are some exceptions to this broad picture. For example, the Government of Tanzania has included a strong focus on conservation and environment in its second poverty reduction strategy. An earlier strategy did not pay adequate attention to the nature of conservation and environment as issues relevant to poverty (Howlett, 2004).

Conservationists concerned with poverty reduction must find ways to engage in the poverty reduction planning process. The first step in this direction could be to start providing the hard economic data on the poverty–conservation connection that economic planners will find useful and convincing. The data emerging from Shinyanga (Case Study 2) may be just the type of information required.[7] Conservationists need to engage in discussion with economic planners to develop a shared understanding of what is useful and possible.

Multiple levels and multiple points of entry

Attempting to work toward conservation and poverty reduction in an integrated way requires working at multiple levels and multiple points of entry. Little can be achieved by working only at the project level or the site level. Concentrating only on the policy level or other institutional levels is also ineffective. Where the problems are caused at different levels and scales then the solutions will be found at multiple levels and scales.

It has often been argued that development works too much at a project level and that a programme approach would be more effective. Increasingly, support from multilateral and bilateral donors to national development is being directed at the programmatic level. While we acknowledge the importance of addressing issues at a national scale, we are very much against an either/or approach to the question of project versus programme. One problem with working too much at a macro-scale is that solutions tend to be informed by homogenizing assumptions – every case is treated as being essentially the same. Even when the main issues are policy concerns or other macro-level issues, it is important to see what happens when policies and solutions are applied on the ground. Good learning projects at the site level are often needed to act as policy 'experiments'. The Lao NTFP Project (Case Study 3) worked that way. It was a flexible, adaptive, learning-oriented project that both informed policy developments (and was widely copied within Lao PDR) and it was able to demonstrate the effects of policy. CAMPFIRE (Chapter 2) also focused on learning and was widely copied. The community-based mangrove management activities at Pred Nai (Case Study 1) followed an action learning approach.

Policy experiments can give feedback on the effects of policy. They can demonstrate how women, children, pastoralists or fisherfolk can all be affected differently by policies and actions, which can allow corrections to be made in the interests of livelihoods, poverty reduction and equity.

Thus there are two reasons for including project- and site-level actions in a broad multilevel approach. One is the need for policy experiments. The other is the need to address complex problems at different levels. An example from Tanzania illustrates this (see Box 5.3).

It is easy to say that initiatives should work at multiple levels (people often say they are doing that), but it is less easy to accomplish this in practice. It is essential to continually monitor changes and issues, to apply progressive contextualization (both up and down) and to amend what we do accordingly. This is adaptive learning or adaptive management.

Box 5.3 Conservation in the Tanga Coastal Zone

In the mid-1990s, IUCN's Eastern Africa Regional Programme established the Tanga Coastal Zone Conservation and Development Programme (TCZCDP) in partnership with the Tanga Regional Secretariat of the United Republic of Tanzania. Through a highly consultative and participatory process, particularly at the local level, the programme helped establish collaborative management areas (CMAs) for coastal fisheries and provided technical input to a national programme of mangrove forest management.

The TCZCDP's two major objectives were: 1) to improve the capacity of district and regional governments to undertake integrated coastal zone management, and 2) to assist communities in using coastal resources in sustainable ways to improve their management and conservation. Coastal fisheries in the Tanga region were seriously depleted due to overfishing and the use of seine nets, which are illegal due to their small mesh and the damage they do to the seabed. Coral reef habitats were also severely degraded through the use of dynamite fishing, also illegal.

Solutions included the establishment of CMAs with associated collaborative management area plans (CMAPs), which closed off certain reefs to fishing. These refuges then export larvae and adults to neighbouring reefs and allow fish populations to recover. In addition, comprehensive patrolling of the waters by an enforcement team comprising district officers and local villagers, in collaboration with the navy, has led to a marked decline in dynamite fishing and the use of seine nets.

The CMAs and the patrolling have led to a steady recovery of the coral reefs. While the prognosis for an increased fish catch and improved conservation of the reefs was good, the long-term sustainability of the approach required changes to national fisheries policy to allow communities to collaboratively manage and take responsibility for their fishery areas. The CMAPs are formally established through village bylaws, but have yet to be formally approved at the national level. TCZCDP's approach has, however, played a vital role in the development of the National Integrated Coastal Environment Management Strategy of Tanzania (January 2003), in the revision of the Fisheries Act, and in the National Mangrove Management Programme. In addition, fisheries officers within the district governments have provided extensive institutional support, along with an understanding of the issues and the capacity to provide extension services to local people and support local management committees to govern their own resources.

Nevertheless, the long-term financial sustainability of this approach is in question if national government does not recognize the value of the CMA approach developed in the Tanga Region. This recognition is vital if funding to districts for local fisheries management initiatives is to increase. Linking sound coastal and marine resource management to poverty alleviation in coastal people is likely to provide a strong message to the United Republic of Tanzania.

Source: Contributed by Bill Jackson and Melita Samoilys of IUCN

Implications of linking poverty reduction and conservation

Based on the discussion in the last two chapters, there are some implications for action. These are presented in the form of guidelines. Where conservation interventions or policies are being promoted in a country or region with high levels of poverty, responsible conservation organizations ought to observe the following guidelines, both because it is ethically desirable to do so and because failure to do so may seriously compromise long-term conservation.

In general

- Know who the poor are. Don't assume that this is already known or obvious. The poor are not a homogeneous mass; poverty manifests itself in different peoples' lives in different ways.
- Determine how different groups of poor people use biological diversity as a local livelihood resource and assess how proposed conservation interventions will affect this.
- Be versatile in the use of conservation tools. Recognize that locally accountable systems of land-use management that encourage diverse and locally adapted approaches to the management of degraded natural resources are a legitimate conservation tool.
- Take responsibility for negotiating equitable outcomes over the use and conservation of natural resources. It is not good enough to ignore this as 'someone else's' problem.
- Build conservation strategies that safeguard biodiversity both for its value as a local livelihood resource and its worth as a national or global or public good.
- Build the capacity of communities not only to protect biodiversity but to use it sustainably. This will include addressing constraints (for example improving poor people's access to markets for natural resource products).
- Ensure that there are ways to identify the social, economic and environmental impacts of interventions. This may include participatory assessment and the establishment of baselines.
- As a general strategy, start by identifying and addressing those policy and institutional constraints that prevent poor people from gaining meaningful access to, and decision-making authority over, natural resources.
- Ensure that biodiversity is built into national development strategies (such as PRSPs) as an opportunity for development and growth aimed specifically at the poor.

Protected areas

- Ensure that the real costs of protected areas – in terms of impacts on rural livelihoods – are provided for and not treated as externalities.

- Look for ways to achieve conservation goals through a landscape approach before assuming that strictly protected areas are the solution.
- Examine other options to conservation, rather than starting with the assumption that protected areas, which require management by the highest competent authority, are the best solution. Instead consider an approach that looks for conservation-focused decentralized land management options that delegate authority to the *lowest competent authority* (consistent with Principle 2 of the ecosystem approach).
- In cases of extremely high conservation value, where other options are not viable, state-controlled protected areas may be the solution.[8] This should not, however, be the default position; it should be limited to sites of national and global importance. In such cases provision must be made for local people, especially the poor, to receive meaningful compensation for the opportunity costs of the protected area to them *and be provided with meaningful alternative livelihood options acceptable to them.*[9]
- Determine the benefits of natural resource use by the rural poor in and around proposed protected areas well before they are gazetted, and ascertain the extent to which protected area restrictions will impose costs on the rural poor. Compensation can then be designed *in collaboration with local stakeholders.*

The guidelines/strategies suggested for protected areas will be controversial to many conservationists. Clearly, protected areas will sometimes be necessary, but many good conservation and livelihood outcomes occur outside them. In fact, attempting to address biodiversity conservation through establishing protected areas alone is doomed to failure, partly because the potential area likely to be allocated for them is necessarily limited. In any case, as conservationists admit, many protected areas exist only on paper anyway. A comprehensive biodiversity conservation strategy must look beyond the sole focus on protected areas.

There are some cases where total protection may be necessary. In such situations, the costs of total protection/exclusion of affected people should be regarded as an intrinsic cost of conservation (like fences and staff salaries). Of course, the same argument applies to natural resource industries (such as mining and forestry), which do not have a good record of addressing the costs of their activities on the poor.

Conclusions

This chapter has identified some of the institutional factors that may help conservation contribute to poverty reduction, either by removing barriers or by providing incentives. These factors include local institutions that more effectively empower the poor in relation to natural resources.

These are some of the key lessons for implementing poverty reduction in conservation:

- It is essential to understand the complexity of different stakeholder interests in both conservation and development issues, and it is essential to ensure that institutional arrangements for handling this complexity are appropriate and relevant to the resource or landscape to be managed.
- There is a need to work at multiple levels and scales.
- Field projects and site-level activities can be very useful as policy experiments and adaptive learning is a valuable way to implement such activities.

Notes

1   It has been argued (Gronow, personal communication) that formalizing (in the sense of recognizing or legalizing) community institutions and organizations often reduces the de facto power of women. Where decision making about resource use remains informal, women often make the important day-to-day decisions. Formalizing decision making often means shifting the process to the level of local politics.

2   According to Tacconi (2006), even if 'democratic decentralization' is implemented, there is no guarantee that it will lead to either forest conservation or poverty reduction. Other policies are required to make decentralization work for these objectives, such as appropriate financial incentives and 'participatory planning, monitoring and evaluation of performance' (p346).

3   In fact, governments often do not want to see too much power over resources devolved to local people because of broader issues of political control, rather than specifically for reasons associated with conservation (Shepherd, personal communication).

4   This does not imply that traditional lecturing may not be efficient at providing information and skills. We are referring solely to training as a means to change attitudes.

5   The English acronymn is ACICAFOC.

6   For a discussion of the characteristics of institutional economics applied to the environment, see Jacobs (1994).

7   The Forests-Poverty Toolkit (originally devised for the World Bank's Program on Forests (PROFOR) by Gill Shepherd and others) is part of an overall package designed to collect information on forest dependence and to use this information to highlight the importance of forests to poverty reduction strategies. The Toolkit uses modified forest-focused participatory rural appraisal techniques to identify levels of forest dependence among richer and poorer local people and as they affect men and women. The Toolkit gathers data on trends over the past 30 years or so and helps villagers to

identify what they think are the key forest problems in their area, and their potential solutions. The Toolkit is being adapted for use in other biomes, and for landscape management activities. The original version of the Toolkit can be downloaded from the PROFOR website at www.profor.info/toolkits. html.

8   There are doubts about just how much displacement can be justified even from a conservation point of view. In a review of the relationship between conservation in protected areas and human displacement, Agrawal and Redford (2007) conclude that protected areas have contributed to the conservation of 'rare species and endangered habitats', but that 'there are very few studies that establish a relationship between displacement of humans from the protected areas and the *marginal* gain such displacement confers on biodiversity conservation' (p14, emphasis original).

9   We recommend compensating people for forgone benefits as well as making provision for alternative livelihoods. Although some people may regard this as double payment for opportunity costs, we would argue that one-off compensation would almost certainly leave people in poverty in the longer term.

6

Linking Conservation and Poverty Reduction

The challenge

This chapter summarizes the main features and key challenges involved in linking conservation with poverty reduction. Not all conservation can contribute to poverty reduction. Some conservation activities appear to have little obvious relationship to poverty and livelihoods (protecting the Antarctic or high seas environment, for example). But where conservation and poverty intersect, conservation can do much more to contribute to poverty reduction, simply because natural resources are important for livelihoods and human wellbeing. Conservation should take poverty and livelihoods more seriously because it can help alleviate a serious global problem and because addressing these issues often makes for better conservation. In cases where conservation has negative effects on the livelihoods of poor people, or where it limits their opportunities for development, we believe there is an ethical imperative to address these impacts.

The connections between poverty and conservation are many and complex. They are rarely simple cause-and-effect relationships. Sometimes there are obvious synergies. Often win–win solutions to poverty and conservation dilemmas are elusive and trade-offs are more realistic outcomes. These outcomes (whether win–win or trade-offs) are not always obvious; sometimes creative approaches must be made to remove constraints and develop synergies. Connections must be made, not simply identified. In many ways linking conservation with poverty reduction is more of an art than a science. Ultimately, the aim is not to achieve perfect outcomes but the best possible outcomes. This was put rather nicely at a 2007 conference on biodiversity for development: 'Don't let the perfect be the enemy of the good' (Najam, quoted in Schei, 2007, p38).

These are some of the characteristics of an approach that links conservation and poverty reduction:

- All interventions must take equity into account in terms of sharing of costs and impacts on the poor. Efforts must be made to address equity issues, including gender equity.
- Interventions should aim for the best possible outcomes, not for unachievable perfect outcomes.
- The specific characteristics of poverty and its relationship to the environment are not homogeneous – they vary according to context. They need to be understood according to their specific context, and their causes and interconnections can be explored through progressive contextualization.
- Win–win outcomes should not be assumed; instead efforts should be made to seek win-more–lose-less outcomes.
- Trade-offs at the landscape scale present opportunities for win-more–lose-less outcomes.
- Where conservation goals are extremely important, and where human costs cannot be met within a landscape or internalized, these associated costs must be seen as part of the real cost of conservation (such as building fences or paying staff). Mechanisms need to be developed to finance these human costs, perhaps by direct payment or compensation. (It is not good enough to say this is someone else's responsibility.)
- Addressing the human costs of conservation implies more than maintaining the status quo in terms of income or subsistence. Poor people need to be empowered so that they can make real development choices.
- The causes of both poverty and biodiversity loss occur at multiple scales and multiple levels. They must be addressed where they occur.
- Most causes of poverty and biodiversity loss are multiple-level and multiple-scale. Multiple points of entry are required.
- Poverty and biodiversity loss are moving targets with complex interactions. Efforts to manage for both poverty and conservation objectives require adaptive learning.

The scope for linking conservation and poverty reduction

Clearly conservation can make only a partial contribution to poverty reduction. The problem is large and primarily a matter for which governments are ultimately responsible and for which most solutions will lie in markets and institutions outside what we normally see as the conservation field. Nevertheless, there are areas where conservation has significant potential for contributing to poverty reduction.

The potential (and ethical requirement) for addressing poverty reduction through conservation does not apply everywhere. It is not appropriate or necessary in cases where there is little poverty or vulnerability to poverty combined with high environmental values and risks. There is, however, scope for conservation to contribute to poverty reduction in a range of different situations with different levels of vulnerability and poverty and different levels of environmental values and risks. Figure 6.1 attempts to illustrate the scope for intervention.

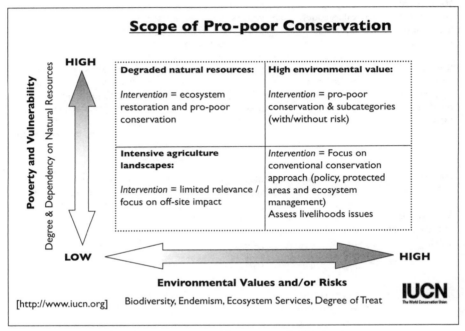

Figure 6.1 *Scope for conservation to address poverty reduction*

Source: IUCN

It is important to recognize the value of restoration of natural resources. Cases such as Pred Nai, Shinyanga and the Senegal River show clearly the importance of landscape restoration as a tool for both improved livelihoods and conservation.

Based on the various dimensions of poverty defined by the World Bank, there are a number of different entry points for agencies wishing to address both poverty and conservation. Different things can be done at site levels and institutional levels. Table 6.1 presents a list of possible activities to address the various dimensions of poverty from a conservation framework.

Table 6.1 *Entry points for implementation*

Dimension of poverty	Entry points	Local/site-level interventions	Policy/political (national/international) interventions
Problem: lack of assets and opportunities **Solution:** provide opportunities, build/restore assets	• employment • value added • access to capital, technology and markets • trade policy • competition policy • resource tenure	• forest restoration • watershed protection • NTFP marketing • improved access to resources and tenure • microcredit programmes • biodiversity-friendly enterprises	• tenure reform • transfer mechanisms to compensate loss and reward stewardship • environment and poverty concerns built into international trade • access and benefit-sharing related to genetic resources • research to improve farm productivity
Problem: lack of power **Solution:** empowerment and access	• participation • democratic decision making • rule of law (equality before the law) • access to information • accountability and transparency	• user groups supported • gender and equity aspects of projects • citizen report cards • power relations that limit access are addressed	• tenure reform • user networks supported • public administrative reform • devolved power to the grassroots • strengthened recognition of cultural identity/indigenous knowledge • enhanced connectivity of rural areas
Problem: vulnerability **Solution:** security	• diversification • insurance • prevention • early warning /prediction	• infrastructure and neighbourhood improvement • diverse livelihood options and low-cost local initiatives to help communities deal with risk of natural disasters • food banks and agricultural cooperatives	• plan for better disaster management with communities • provide access rights to diverse resources in protected areas
Problem: lack of capability **Solution:** enhance capability	• literacy • health • provision of basic services • access to information	• environmental sanitation projects • skills development • build capacity of/revive local institutions	• research on diseases that affect the poor • formal and non-formal education programmes • enhanced connectivity of rural areas

A learning approach

We would like to make it clear that this is not intended to be a prescriptive how-to book. As far as a comprehensive approach to linking poverty reduction and conservation is concerned, nobody knows exactly 'how to' based on a wide range of successful experiences. Nevertheless, conservation must treat livelihoods and poverty more seriously for ethical reasons and there is a great deal of evidence to show that positive outcomes are often possible. Although a comprehensive and well-tested approach has not been widely applied, there is considerable understanding of fields such as institutional change, landscape management and the sociology of development that suggest ways to move ahead.

Despite the work that has been done in ICDPs, CBNRM and related approaches, linking conservation with poverty reduction and livelihoods has not yet been successful on a large scale. There have been calls for evidence-based approaches to conservation and many conservationists point out (especially in informal discussion) that there is little empirical evidence to show the result of interventions, in terms of either conservation or poverty. To a considerable extent this is true, although one reason for the uncertainty may be that many people expect to be able to draw broad generalizations about causal relationships. Cause-and-effect relationships depend on contextual factors, however, and intervening factors, such as institutional arrangements (at a variety of levels), can have a strong influence on the effect of interventions.

A great deal can be learned from earlier efforts in conservation and rural development. Many sociological lessons suggest what might plausibly work. Some of these ideas are explored here. There is much that seems promising but much that remains to be tested. We have aimed to contribute to the discussion and experimentation that has involved many of our colleagues.

For people and organizations working in poverty reduction and conservation – whether they call it community forestry, integrated conservation and development or whatever – the challenge is to continually evaluate what is done and to question its impacts on conservation and the poor. Practitioners must ask how they have affected specific groups (women, fisherfolk, farmers) and why these impacts have happened. This sort of evaluation can help to change what is not working or is counterproductive and can validate ideas, approaches and strategies for future application.

In complex and uncertain contexts and especially where there is continual change, flexible and adaptive approaches, such as adaptive management and action research, are imperative. In the case of conservation that aims to achieve both conservation and livelihood objectives, it is particularly important to continually assess the impacts of actions against expressed goals. What is really happening to the poor? What is really happening to biodiversity? What have the impacts been? Obviously there is a need for systematic collection of economic data, disaggregated to show the impacts on specific groups. There is also a need for participatory assessment and participatory evaluation. Ultimately, nobody is better qualified to tell what has happened to the rural poor than the people themselves.

Conclusion

This book has not proposed any grand scheme for linking conservation and poverty reduction. It has argued that a landscape approach that moves beyond an emphasis on sites and a focus on protected areas is an important tool. It has also stressed the importance of dealing with issues of power. The book has looked at some experiences and ideas that seem likely to assist better-informed efforts to address these linked issues of poverty reduction and conservation.

The challenge is the need to make an explicit commitment to both conservation and poverty reduction goals. Conservationists often argue that a healthy environment is necessary for the quality of human life. Conservation can contribute to this, not just in a global sense but for the rural people who depend directly on the environment and often pay for the global quality of life with reduced wellbeing and limited opportunities.

References

ACOFOP (Asociación de Comunidades Forestales de Petén) (2004) 'Carta abierta al sr. presidente de la República de Guatemala, Lic. Oscar Bergar Perdomo, Magistrados de la Corte de Constitucionalidad y Miembros del Congreso' [Open letter to the President of the Republic of Guatemala], *Prensa Libre*, 26 January, www.acofop.org, accessed 26 January 2004

ACOFOP (2005) 'Representamos al proyecto forestal comunitario más grande del mundo', www.acofop.org, accessed 4 February 2005

Adams, J. S. and McShane, T. O. (1992) *The Myth of Wild Africa: Conservation Without Illusion*, The University of California Press, Berkeley, Los Angeles and London

Adams, W. M. (1990) *Green Development: Environment and Sustainability in the Third World*, Routledge, London

Agrawal, A. (1997) 'Community in conservation: Beyond enchantment and disenchantment', CDF Discussion Paper, Conservation and Development Forum, University of Florida, Gainsville, FL

Agrawal, A. and Redford, K. H. (2007) 'Conservation and development', in K. H. Redford and E. Fearn (eds) *Protected Areas and Human Displacement: A Conservation Perspective*, Working Paper No 29, Wildlife Conservation Society, Bronx, New York, pp4–15

Alchian, A. A. (1987) 'Property rights', in J. Eatwell, M. Milgate, and P. Newman (eds) *The New Palgrave: A Dictionary of Economics*, London, Macmillan

Anderson, J., Clement, J. and Crowder, L. V. (1998) 'Accommodating conflicting interests in forestry: Concepts emerging from pluralism', *Unasylva*, vol 49, no 3, pp3–10

Angelsen, A. and Kaimowitz, D. (1999) 'Rethinking the causes of deforestation; Lessons from economic models', *The World Bank Research Observer*, vol 14, no 1, pp73–98

Angelsen, A. and Wunder, S. (2003) 'Exploring the forest–poverty link: Key concepts, issues and research implications', CIFOR Occasional Paper No 40, Center for International Forestry Research, Bogor, Indonesia

Arnstein, S. R. (1969) 'A ladder of citizen participation', *Journal of the American Institute of Planners*, vol 35, pp216–224

Bader, J. C., Lamagat, J.-P. and Guiguen, N. (2003) 'Gestion du barrage de Manantali sur le Fleuve Sénégal: Analyse quantitative d'un conflit d'objectifs', *Journal des Sciences Hydrologiques*, vol 48, pp525–538

Barrett, C. B. and Arcese, P. (1995) 'Are integrated conservation-development projects (ICDPs) sustainable? On the conservation of large mammals in sub-Saharan Africa', *World Development*, vol 23, pp1073–1084

Barrow, E. G. C. (1996) *The Drylands of Africa: Local Participation in Tree Management*, Initiatives Publishers, Nairobi

Barrow, E. G. C. (2000) *Rhetoric or Reality?: A Review of Community Conservation Policy and Practice in East Africa*, Evaluating Eden Series No 5, International Institute for Environment and Development (IIED), London

Barrow, E. G. C. and Mlenge, W. (2003) 'Trees as key to pastoralist risk management in semi-arid landscapes in Shinyanga, Tanzania and Turkana, Kenya', International Conference on Rural Livelihoods, Forest and Biodiversity, CIFOR, Bonn, Germany, 19–23 May

Barrow, E. G. C. and Murphree, M. (2001) 'Community conservation from concept to practice', in D. Hulme and M. Murphree (eds) *African Wildlife and Livelihoods: The Promise and Practice of Community Conservation*, James Currey, Oxford

Barrow, E. G. C., Brandstrom, P., Kabelele, M. and Kikula, I. (1988) 'Soil conservation and afforestation in Shinyanga Region: Potentials and constraints', Mission Report to NORAD, Norad, Dar-es-Salaam, Tanzania

Barrow, E. G. C., Clarke, J., Grundy, I., Kamugisha, J. R. and Tessema, Y. (2002) 'Analysis of stakeholder power and responsibilities in community involvement in forest management in Eastern and Southern Africa', IUCN Eastern African Office, Nairobi

Barrow, E. G. C., Gichohi, H. and Infield, M. (2000) 'Rhetoric or Reality? A review of community conservation policy and practice in East Africa', *Evaluating Eden Series* No 5, IIED, London, p184

Barrow, E. G. C., Fry, P. and Lugeye, S. (1992) 'Hifadhi ardhi Shinyanga (HASHI)', Evaluation Report for Ministry of Tourism, Natural Resources and Environment, United Republic of Tanzania and Norwegian Agency for International Development, Dar-es-Salaam

Berkes, F. (1989) *Common Property Resources: Ecology and Community-Based Sustainable Development*, Helhaven Press, London

Blaikie, P. (2006) 'Is small really beautiful? Community-based natural resource management in Malawi and Botswana', *World Development*, vol 34, no 11, pp1942–1957

Blaikie, P. and Brookfield, H. (1987) *Land Degradation and Society*, Routledge, London

Bond, I. (2001) 'CAMPFIRE and the incentives for institutional change', in D. Hulme and M. Murphree (eds) *African Wildlife and Livelihoods: The Promise and Practice of Community Conservation*, James Currey, Oxford

Borrini-Feyerabend, G. (ed) (1997) *Beyond Fences: Seeking Social Sustainability in Conservation*, 2 vols, IUCN, Gland, Switzerland

Brandon, K. E. and Wells, M. (1992) 'Planning for people and parks: Design dilemmas', *World Development*, vol 20, no 4, pp557–570

Bray, D. B., Durán, E., Ramos, V. H., Mas, J.-F., Velázquez, A., McNab, R. B., Barry, D. and Radachowsky, J. (forthcoming) 'Tropical deforestation, community forests, and protected areas in the Maya Forest' submitted to *Ecology and Society*, September 2007

Brockington, D. (2003) 'Injustice and conservation: Is "local support" necessary for sustainable protected areas?', *Policy Matters*, vol 12, pp22–30

Brockington, D. and Igoe, J. (2006) 'Eviction for conservation: A global overview', *Conservation and Society*, vol 4, no 3, pp424–470

Brown, K. (2003) 'Integrating conservation and development: A case of institutional misfit', *Frontiers in Ecology and the Environment*, vol 1, no 9, pp479–487

Brown, M. (1991) *Buffer Zone Management in Africa*, The PVO-NGO/NRMS Project, Washington DC

Buck, L. B., Geisler, C. C., Schelhas, J. and Wollenberg, E. (eds) (2001) *Biological Diversity: Balancing Interests Through Adaptive Collaborative Management*, CRC Press, Boca Raton, Florida

Carney, D., Drinkwater, M., Rusinow, T., Neefjes, K., Wanmali, S. and Singh, N. (1999) *Livelihood Approaches Compared: A Brief Comparison of the Livelihoods Approaches of the UK Department for International Development (DFID), CARE, Oxfam and the United Nations Development Programme*, DFID, London

Carwardine, M. (1990) *The WWF Environment Handbook*, Macdonald Co, London

Chambers, R. (1988) *Poverty in India: Concepts, Research and Reality*, IDS Discussion Paper 241, Institute of Development Studies, Brighton

Chambers, R. and Conway, G. (1992) *Sustainable Rural Livelihoods: Practical Concepts for the 21st Century,* IDS Discussion Paper 296, IDS, Brighton

Chase, A. (1987) *Playing God in Yellowstone: The Destruction of America's First National Park,* Harcourt Brace, New York

Colchester, M. (1992) *Sustaining the Forests: The Community-Based Approach in South and South-East Asia,* UNRISD Discussion Paper No 35, Geneva, Switzerland

Colchester, M. (1994) *Salvaging Nature: Indigenous People, Protected Areas and Biodiversity Conservation,* UNRISD Discussion Paper No 55, Geneva, Switzerland

Colchester, M. and Lohmann, L. (eds) (1993) *The Struggle for Land and the Fate of the Forests,* The World Rainforest Movement, *The Ecologist* and Zed Books, Dorset, Penang and London

Colchester, M., Apte, T., Laforge, M., Mandondo, A. and Pathak, N. (2003) *Bridging the Gap: Communities, Forests and International Networks,* CIFOR Occasional Paper No 41, Center for International Forestry Research, Bogor, Indonesia

Cole, M. A. and Neumayer, E. (2005) 'Economic growth and the environment in developing countries: What are the implications of the environmental Kuznets curve?', in P. Dauvergne (ed) *International Handbook of Environmental Politics,* Edward Elgar Publishing, Cheltenham and Northampton

Colfer, C. J. P., Prabhu, R., Gunter, P. M., McDougall, C., Porro, N. M. and Porro, R. (1999) *Who Counts Most? Assessing Human Well-Being in Sustainable Forest Management,* C and I Toolbox Series No 8, Center for International Forestry Research, Bogor, Indonesia

CONAP (1994) *Normas de Adjudicación de Concesiones,* Consejo Nacional de Areas Protegidas, Guatemala City

Craig, D. and Porter, D. (2003) 'Poverty reduction strategy papers: A new convergence', *World Development,* vol 31, no 1, pp53–69

Croll, E. and Parkin, D. (eds) (1992) *Bush Base, Forest Farm: Culture, Environment and Development,* Routledge, London

Cronkleton, P., Taylor, P. L., Stone-Jovicich, S., Schmink, M. and Barry, D. (2008) *Environmental Governance and the Emergence of Forest-based Social Movements,* CIFOR Occasional Paper No 49, Bogor, Indonesia

Dasmann, R. (1976) 'National parks, nature conservation and future primitive', *The Ecologist,* vol 6, no 5, pp164–167

Dasmann, R. (1984) 'The relationship between protected areas and indigenous people', in J. McNeely and K. R. Miller (eds) *National Parks, Conservation and Development: The Role of Protected Areas in Sustaining Society,* Smithsonian International Press, Washington DC

Dechaineux, R. (2001) 'Role of forest food resources in village livelihood systems: A study of three villages in Salavan Province, Lao PDR', February, unpublished project report, NTFP Project, IUCN/ NAFRI, Vientiane, Lao PDR

de Soto, H. (2000) *The Mystery of Capital: Why Capitalism Triumphs in the West and Fails Everywhere Else,* Basic Books, New York

di Castri, F. (1976) 'International, interdisciplinary research in ecology: Some problems of organization and execution: The case of the Man and Biosphere (MAB) Programme', *Human Ecology,* vol 4, pp235–246

DFID (Department for International Development) (2002) *Wildlife and Poverty Study,* prepared by the Livestock and Wildlife Advisory Group, Rural Livelihoods Department, DFID, London

DOF and NTFP Project (2000) *A Study of the Downstream Impacts of the Yali Falls Dam in the Se San River Basin in Ratanakiri Province, Northeast Cambodia,* prepared by the Fisheries Office, Ratanakiri Province in Cooperation with the Non-Timber Forest Products Project, Ratanakiri Province, May 29, available in 'Negotiating River Basin Management: Lessons from the Mekong', CD-Rom produced by the Australian Mekong Resource Centre (AMRC), University of Sydney, 2003

Donovan, D., Mounday, B., Souvanthalysith, S. and Gilmour, D. (1998) 'Sustainable utilisation of non-timber forest products in Lao PDR', report of Mid-Term Review Mission, NTFP Project, IUCN/NAFRI, May

Dove, M. (1993) 'A revisionist view of tropical deforestation and development', *Environmental Conservation*, vol 20, no 1, pp17–24

Duvail, S. and Hamerlynck, O. (2003) 'Hydraulic modelling as a tool for the joint management of a restored wetland: Sharing the benefits of managed flood releases from the Diama dam reservoir', *Hydrology and Earth System Sciences*, vol 7, pp133–146

Ellen, R. (1986) 'What Black Elk left unsaid: On the illusory images of green primitivism', *Anthropology Today*, vol 2, no 6, pp8–12

Espinosa, C. (2004) *Unveiling Difference: Finding a Balance*, IUCN Social Policy Program and IUCN Regional Office for South America, Gland and Quito

Fairhead, J. and Leach, M. (1995) 'False forest history, complicit social analysis: Rethinking some West African environmental narratives', *World Development*, vol 23, no 6, pp1023–1035

Fairhead, J. and Leach, M. (1996) *Misreading the African Landscape: Society and Ecology in a Forest-Savanna Mosaic*, Cambridge University Press, Cambridge, New York and Melbourne

Fairhead, J. and Leach, M. (1998) *Reframing Deforestation, Global Analysis and Local Realities*, Routledge, London

Fisher, R. and Ury, W. (1981) *Getting to Yes: Negotiating Agreement Without Giving In*, Houghton Mifflin, Boston

Fisher, R. J. (1989) *Indigenous Systems of Common Property Forest Management in Nepal*, Working Paper No 18, East-West Environment and Policy Institute, East-West Center, Honolulu

Fisher, R. J. (1994) 'Indigenous forest management in Nepal: Why common property is not a problem', in M. Allen (ed) *Anthropology of Nepal: People, Problems and Processes*, Mandala Book Point, Kathmandu

Fisher, R. J. (1995) *Collaborative Management of Forests for Conservation and Development*, WWF International and IUCN, Gland, Switzerland

Fisher, R. J. (1999) 'Devolution and decentralization of forest management in Asia and the Pacific', *Unasylva*, vol 50, no 4, pp3–5

Fisher, R. J. (2000) 'Poverty alleviation and forests: Experiences from Asia', paper prepared for Forest Ecospaces, Biodiversity and Environmental Security Workshop held at the IUCN World Conservation Congress, 4–11 October, Amman, Jordan

Fisher, R. J. (2003) 'Innovations, persistence and change: Reflections on the state of community forestry', in RECOFTC and FAO (eds) *Community Forestry: Current Innovations and Experiences*, Regional Community Forestry Training Center and Food and Agricultural Organization of the United Nations, Bangkok

Fisher, R. J., Prabhu, R. and McDougall, C. (eds) (2007) *Adaptive Collaborative Management of Community Forests in Asia: Experiences from Nepal, Indonesia and the Philippines*, Center for International Forestry Research, Bogor, Indonesia

Fraval, P., Bader, J.-C., Mané, L. K., David-Benz, H., Lamagat, J.-P. and Diagne, O. (2002) 'The quest for integrated and sustainable water management in the Senegal River Valley', paper presented at the 5th Interregional Conference on Environment and Water, Envirowater, EIER ETSHER, 5–8 November, Ouagadougou, Burkina Faso

General Assembly of the United Nations (2005) *2005 World Summit Outcome*, Resolution 60/1, United Nations, New York

Ghimire, K. and Pimbert, M. (eds) (1997) *Social Change and Conservation: Environmental Politics and Impacts of National Parks and Protected Areas*, Earthscan, London

Gilmour, D. A. and Fisher, R. J. (1991) *Villagers, Forests and Foresters: The Philosophy, Process and Practice of Community Forestry in Nepal*, Sahayogi Press, Kathmandu

Gilmour, D., Malla, Y. and Nurse, M. (2004) *Linkages Between Community Forestry and Poverty*, Regional Community Forestry Center for Asia and the Pacific, Bangkok

Gómez, I. and Méndez, V. E. (2005) *Análisis de Contexto: El Caso de la Asociación de Comunidades Forestales de Petén (ACOFOP)*, PRISMA, San Salvador, El Salvador

Gomez-Pompa, A. and Kaus, A. (1992) 'Taming the wilderness myth', *Bioscience*, vol 42, no 4, pp271–279

Government of Western Australia (2005) *Ord Final Agreement*, Office of Native Title, Government of Western Australia, Perth; www.nativetitle.wa.gov.au/agreements_OrdFinalAgreement.aspx, accessed 2 May 2008

Gretzinger, S. P. (1998) 'Community forest concessions: An economic alternative for the Maya Biosphere Reserve in the Petén, Guatemala', in R. B. Primack, D. Bray, H. A. Galletti and I. Ponciano (eds) *Timber, Tourists, and Temples: Conservation and Development in the Maya Forest of Belize, Guatemala, and Mexico*, Island Press, Covelo, CA

Guha, R. (1989) 'Radical American environmentalism and wilderness preservation: A Third World critique', *Environmental Ethics*, vol 11, pp71–83

Guha, R. and Martinez-Alier, J. (1997) *Varieties of Environmentalism, Essays North and South*, Earthscan, London

Hamerlynck, O. and Duvail, S. (2003) *The Rehabilitation of the Delta of the Senegal River in Mauritania: Fielding the Ecosystem Approach*, IUCN, Gland, Switzerland and Cambridge, UK

Hamerlynck, O., Duvail, S., Messaoud, B. and Benmergui, M. (2005) 'The restoration of the delta of the Lower Delta of the Senegal River, Mauritania (1994–2004)', in J. J. Symoens (ed) *Coastal Ecosystems of West Africa, Biological Diversity – Resources – Conservation*, Proceedings of the Conference at the Belgian Academy of Sciences, 15–16 February, Brussels, Belgium

Hanmer, L., Pyatt, G. and White, H. (1999) 'What do the World Bank poverty assessments teach us about poverty in sub-Saharan Africa?', *Development and Change*, vol 30, no 4, pp795–823

Hardin, G. (1968) 'The tragedy of the commons', *Science*, vol 162, pp1243–1248

Hendy, C. R. C. (1980) *Livestock Production in Tabora Region*, Tabora Rural Integrated Development Programme Land-Use Component and Land Resources Development Centre, Tanzania and London

Hillaby, J. (1961) 'Conservation in Africa: A crucial conference', *New Scientist*, vol 11, no 250, pp536–538

Howlett, D. (2004) 'Lessons from Tanzania on mainstreaming environment into the new poverty reduction strategy', in D. Roe (ed) *The Millennium Development Goals and Conservation: Managing Nature's Wealth for Society's Health*, International Institute for Environment and Development, London

Hulme, D. and Murphree, M. (eds) (2001) *African Wildlife and Livelihoods: The Promise and Performance of Community Conservation*, James Currey, Oxford

IFAD (International Fund for Agricultural Development) (2002) *Enabling the Rural Poor to Overcome their Poverty: Strategic Framework for IFAD 2002–2006*, IFAD, Rome

Ingles, A. and Hicks, E. (2002) 'A review of the context for poverty reduction and forest conservation in Lao PDR, and a preliminary look at IUCN's NTFP Project', presentation at IUCN 3I-C Project Core Team Meeting, 24–26 June, Khao Yai, Thailand

Ingles, A. and Hicks, E. (2004) 'Natural wealth: A study for linking poverty reduction with forest conservation in Lao PDR', in J. E. Morris, E. Hicks, A. Ingles and S. Ketpanh (eds) (2004) *Linking Poverty Reduction with Forest Conservation: Case Studies from Lao PDR*, IUCN, Bangkok

Ingles, A. and Karki, S. (2001) 'Project completion report', NAFRI-IUCN NTFP Project, Vientiane

Ingles, A., Ketpanh, S., Inglis, A. and Manivong, K. (2006) 'Scaling sideways and up-ways: Identifying factors that affect the adoption of forest-based livelihoods development interventions in Lao PDR', unpublished report, IUCN, Bangkok

IUCN (The International Union for Conservation of Nature) (2003) *The Durban Accord*, World Parks Congress 2003, IUCN, Durban

IUCN/UNEP/WWF (The International Union for Conservation of Nature/United Nations Environment Programme/World Wide Fund for Nature) (1980) *World Conservation Strategy: Living Resource Conservation for Sustainable Development*, IUCN/UNEP/WWF, Gland, Switzerland

IUCN/UNEP/WWF (1991) *Caring for the Earth: A Strategy for Sustainable Living*, IUCN/UNEP/WWF, Gland, Switzerland

IWGIA (International Work Group for Indigenous Affairs) (1996) *Indigenous Peoples, Forest and Biodiversity*, International Alliance of Indigenous-Tribal Peoples of the Tropical Forests and the IWGIA, London

Jackson, W. J. and. Ingles, A. W. (1994) *Developing Rural Communities and Conserving The Biodiversity Of Nepal's Forests Through Community Forestry*, proceedings of a seminar on community development and conservation of forest biodiversity through community forestry, 26–28 October, Bangkok, Thailand

Jacobs, M. (1994) 'The limits to neoclassicism: Towards an institutional environmental economics', in M. Redclift and T. Benton (eds) *Social Theory and the Global Environment*, Routledge, London and New York

Jeanrenaud, S. (2002) *People-Oriented Approaches in Global Conservation: Is the Leopard Changing its Spots?*, International Institute for Environment and Development and Institute for Development Studies, London and Brighton

Kaale, B. and Gillusson, R. (1985) *Plan for Planting and Conservation of Trees in Shinyanga Region, 1986–2010*, Ministry of Natural Resources and Tourism, Dar-es-Salaam

Kaale, B., Mlenge, W. and Barrow, E. G. C. (2002) *The Potential of Ngitili for Forest Landscape Restoration in Shinyanga Region: A Tanzania Case Study*, International Expert Meeting on Forest Landscape Restoration, Costa Rica

Kaewkuntee, D. (2006) 'Land tenure, land conflicts and post tsunami relocation in Thailand', *Mekong Update & Dialogue*, vol 9, no 2, pp2–5

Kemf, E. (ed) (1993) *The Law of the Mother*, Sierra Club Books, San Francisco

Kerario, E. J. and Nanai, K. (1995) *Desertification Control in Tanzania*, SADC-ELMS, Lesotho

Kilahama, F. B. (1994) 'Indigenous technical knowledge: A vital tool for rural extension strategies. A case study from Shinyanga Region, Tanzania', *Forest Trees and People*, vol 24, pp30–35

Kimberley Land Council (2004) *From Dispossession to Continued Social and Economic Marginalisation: An Aboriginal Social and Economic Impact Assessment of the Ord River Irrigation Project Stage 1*, March, Kimberley Land Council, Broome, Western Australia

Kunstadter, P., Chapman, E. C. and Sabhasri, S. (eds) (1978) *Farmers in the Forest: Economic Development and Marginal Agriculture in Northern Thailand*, East–West Center, Honolulu

Lara, S. (undated a) *Millenium Development Goals: Gender Makes the Difference*, IUCN Fact Sheet, IUCN, Gland, Switzerland

Lara, S. (undated b) *Poverty and Environment: Gender Makes the Difference*, IUCN Fact Sheet, IUCN, Gland, Switzerland

Leach, M., Mearns, R. and Scoones, I. (1997) *Environmental Entitlements: A Framework for Understanding the Institutional Dynamics of Environmental Change*, IDS Discussion Paper 359, Institute of Development Studies, University of Sussex, Brighton

Leach, M., Mearns, R. and Scoones, I. (1999) 'Environmental entitlements: Dynamics and institutions in community based natural resource management', *World Development*, vol 27, pp225–247

Locke, C. (1999) 'Constructing a gender policy for joint forest management in India', *Development and Change*, vol 30, pp265–285

Lohmann, L. (1991) 'Who defends biological diversity?', *The Ecologist*, vol 21, no 1, pp5–13

Loth, P. (ed) (2004) *The Return of the Water: Restoring the Waza Logone Floodplain in Cameroon*, IUCN, Gland, Switzerland and Cambridge, UK

MacKay, F. (2002) *Addressing Past Wrongs. Indigenous Peoples and Protected Areas: The Right to Restitution of Lands and Resources*, FPP Occasional Paper, Forest Peoples Programme, Moreton-in-Marsh, UK

Maginnis, S., Jackson, W. and Dudley, N. (2004) 'Conservation landscapes: Whose landscapes? Whose trade-offs?', in T. O. McShane and M. P. Wells (eds) *Getting Biodiversity Projects to Work: Towards More Effective Conservation and Development*, Columbia University Press, New York

Mainka, S., McNeely, J. and Jackson, B. (2005) *Depend on Nature: Ecosystems Services Supporting Human Livelihoods*, IUCN, Gland, Switzerland

Malcolm, D. W. (1953) *Sukumaland, An African People and Their Country: A Study of Land Use in Tanzania*, Oxford University Press, London

Malla, Y. B. (2000) 'Impact of community forestry on rural livelihoods and food security', *Unasylva*, vol 202, no 52, pp 37–45

Maro, R. S. (1995) *In situ Conservation of Natural Vegetation for Sustainable Production in Agro-Pastoral Systems: A Case Study of Shinyanga, Tanzania,* Centre for International Environment and Development Studies and Agriculture, University of Norway, Aas and Noragric

Maro, R. S. (1997) *Human Development Report for Shinyanga Region: Cotton-Sector Study,* Economic Research Bureau, Dar-es-Salaam

Maxwell, S. (2003) 'Heaven or hubris: Reflections on the new "New Poverty Agenda", *Development Policy Review,* vol 21, no 1, pp5–25

McCormick, J. (1995) *The Global Environmental Movement,* second edition, Wiley, Chichester

McLean, J. and Straede, S. (2003) 'Conservation, relocation and the paradigms of park and people management: A case study of Padampur villages and the Royal Chitwan National Park, Nepal', *Society and Natural Resources,* vol 16, pp509–526

McNeely, J. and Pitt, D. (eds) (1985) *Culture and Conservation: The Human Dimension in Environmental Planning,* Croon Helm, Kent

McShane, T. O. (2003) 'The devil in the detail of biodiversity conservation', *Conservation Biology,* vol 17, pp1–3

McShane, T. and Wells, M. (eds) (2004) *Getting Biodiversity Projects to Work: Towards More Effective Conservation and Development,* Columbia University Press, New York

Meusch, E., Yhoung-Aree, J., Friend, R. and Funge-Smith, S. (2003) *The Role and Nutritional Value of Aquatic Resources in the Livelihoods of Rural People: A Participatory Assessment in Attapeu Province, Lao PDR,* RAP Publication 2003/11, Food and Agriculture Organization of the United Nations, Regional Office for Asia and the Pacific, Bangkok

Millennium Ecosystem Assessment (2005) *Ecosystems and Human Well-being: Synthesis,* Island Press, Washington DC

Milton, K. (ed) (1993) *Environmentalism: The View from Anthropology,* ASA Monographs, Routledge, London

Ministry of Community Development (1996) *Community Development Policy,* The United Republic of Tanzania, Dar-es-Salaam

Monela, G. C., Chamshama, S. A. O., Mwaipopo, R. and Gamassa, D. M. (2004) *A Study on the Social, Economic and Environmental Impacts of Forest Landscape Restoration in Shinyanga Region, Tanzania,* Ministry of Natural Resources and Tourism and IUCN Eastern Africa Regional Office, Tanzania

Monterroso, I. and Barry, D. (2007) 'Community-based forestry and the changes in tenure and access rights in the Mayan Biosphere Reserve, Guatemala', paper presented at International Conference, Poverty Reduction and Forests: Tenure, Market and Policy Reforms, 3–7 September, Regional Community Forestry Training Centre for Asia and the Pacific (RECOFTC), Bangkok

Moulaye, Z. S. A. (2004) *Evaluation de l'impact économique du Parc National du Diawling,* UICN PND DGIS, Nouakchott, Mauritania

Murphree, M. W. (1993) *Communities as Resource Management Institutions,* Gatekeeper Series No 36, International Institute for Environment and Development, London

Murphree, M. W. (1996) 'Approaches to community participation', in Overseas Development Administration (ed) *African Wildlife Policy Consultation: Final Report of the Consultation,* Overseas Development Administration, London

Narayan, D., Chambers, R., Shah, M. K. and Petesch, P. (2000) *Voices of the Poor: Crying Out for Change,* Oxford University Press, Oxford

Nicholson, M. (1981) 'The first World Conservation Lecture', presented at the Royal Institution, 12 March, IUCN, Gland

Nittler, J. and Tschinkel, H. (2005) 'Manejo comunitário del bosque en la Reserva Maya de la Biosfera de Guatemala: Protección mediante ganancias', [Community forest management in Maya Biosphere Reserve of Guatemala: Protection through income], unpublished report, University of Georgia, Watkinsville, GA

Oates, J. F. (1999) *Myth and Reality in the Rain Forest: How Conservation Strategies are Failing in West Africa,* University of California Press, Berkeley and London

Okoth-Owiro, P. (1988) 'Land tenure and land-use legislation in agroforestry development', in D. D. Thomas, E. K. Biamah, A. M. Kilewe, L. Lundgren and B. Mochoge (eds) *Soil Conservation in Kenya: Proceedings of the Third International Workshop*, Department of Agricultural Engineering, University of Nairobi, Nairobi

Ostrom, E. (1990) *Governing the Commons: The Evolution of Institutions for Collective Action*, Cambridge University Press, New York

Otsyina, R., Minae, S. and Asenga, D. (1993) *The Potential of* Ngitili *as a Traditional Agroforestry System among the Sukuma of Tanzania*, ICRAF, Nairobi

Pagiola, S., Arcenas, A. and Latais, G. P. (2004) 'Can payments for environmental services help reduce poverty? An exploration of the issues and the evidence to date from Latin America', *World Development*, vol 33, no 2, pp237–253

Peet, R. and Watts, M. (eds) (1996) *Liberation Ecologies: Environment, Development, Social Movements*, Routledge, London

People–Environment Partnership (2005) *Investing in Environmental Wealth for Poverty Reduction*, jointly prepared by staff from UNDP, UNEP, IIED, IUCN and WRI on behalf of the Poverty–Environment Partnership, United Nations Development Programme, New York

Pimbert, M. and Gujja, B. (1997) 'Village voices challenging wetland management policies: Experiences in participatory rural appraisal from India and Pakistan', *Natural Resources*, vol 33, no 1, pp34–42

Pimbert, M. and Pretty, J. (1995). *Parks, People and Professionals: Putting Participation into Protected Area Management*, UNRISD Discussion Paper No 57, UNRISD, IIED, WWF, Geneva

Pirot, J.-Y., Meynell, P. J. and Elder, D. (2000) *Ecosystem Management: Lessons from Around the World: A Guide for Development and Conservation Practitioners*, IUCN, Gland and Cambridge

Poffenberger, M. and McGean. B. (1996) *Village Voices, Village Choices: Joint Forest Management in India*, Oxford University Press, New York

Posey, D. (1985), 'Indigenous management of tropical forest ecosystems: The case of the Kayapo Indians of the Brazilian Amazon', *Agroforestry Systems*, vol 3, no 2, pp139–158

Radachowski, J. (2004) 'Effects of certified logging on wildlife in community and industrial forest concessions of northern Guatemala', unpublished report to Wildlife Conservation Society, CONAP, USAID, FIPA, Guatemala City

Ribot, J. C. (2002) *Democratic Decentralization of Natural Resources: Institutionalizing Popular Participation*, World Resources Institute, Washington DC

Robinson, J. G. (1999) 'The limits to caring: Sustainable living and the loss of biodiversity', *Conservation Biology*, vol 7, no 1, pp20–28

Rodda, A. (1991) *Women and the Environment*, Zed Books, London and New Jersey

Roe, D. (ed) (2004) *The Millenium Development Goals and Conservation: Managing Nature's Wealth for Society's Health*, International Institute for Environment and Development, London

Roe, D. and Elliott, J. (2004) 'Poverty reduction and biodiversity conservation: rebuilding the bridges', *Oryx*, vol 38, no 2, pp137–139

Roney, J., Kunen, J. and Donald, M. (undated) 'Evaluación arqueológico. Resumen ejecutivo' [Archaelogical evaluation, executive summary], unpublished report submitted to USAID, Guatemala City

Sanderson, S. E. and Redford, K. (2003) 'Contested relationships between biodiversity conservation and poverty alleviation', *Oryx*, vol 37, no 4, pp389–390

Sarin, M. (1998) *Who is Gaining? Who is Losing? Gender and Equity Concerns in Joint Forest Management*, Society for Promotion of Wastelands Development, New Delhi

Sayer, J. A. (1995) *Science and International Nature Conservation*, CIFOR Occasional Paper No 4, Centre for International Forestry Research, Jakarta

Scanlon, J., Cassar, A. and Nemes, N. (2004) *Water as a Human Right?*, Environmental Policy and Law Paper No 51, IUCN, Gland

Schei, P. (2007) 'Chairman's report: The Trondheim/UN Conference on Ecosystems and People – Biodiversity for Development – The road to 2010 and beyond', 29 October–2 November, Norwegian Directorate for Nature Management, Trondheim, Norway

Scherl, L. M., Wilson, A., Wild, R., Blochus, J., Franks, P., McNeeley, J. A. and McShane, T. O.

(2004) *Can Protected Areas Contribute to Poverty Reduction? Opportunities and Limitations,* IUCN, Cambridge and Gland

Sen, A. (1999) *Development as Freedom,* Oxford University Press, Oxford and New York

Shepherd, G. (2004) *The Ecosystem Approach: Five Steps to Implementation,* IUCN, Gland and Cambridge

Shepherd, G. (2008) 'Forest restoration, rights and power: What's going wrong in the *ngitili* forests of Shinyanga?', *ArborVitae,* vol 36, p3

Shepherd, G., Shanks, E. and Hobley, M. (1991) *National Experiences in managing Tropical and Sub tropical Dry Forests: Representative Case Studies Illustrating Successes, Shortcomings and Promising Opportunities for National Level Planning of Forest Management,* ODI, London

Smith, R. D. and Maltby, E. (2003) *Using the Ecosystem Approach to Implement the Convention on Biological Diversity: Key Issues and Case Studies,* IUCN, Gland and Cambridge

Sudmeier-Rieux, K., Masundire, H., Rizvi, A. and Rietbergen, S. (eds) (2006) *Ecosystems, Livelihoods and Disasters: An Integrated Approach to Disaster Risk Management,* Ecosystem Management Series No 4, IUCN, Gland and Cambridge

Sutherland, W. J., Pullin, A. S., Dolman, P. M. and Knight, T. M. (2004) 'The need for evidence-based conservation', *Trends in Ecology and Evolution,* vol 19, no 6, pp305–308

Tacconi, L. (2006) 'Decentralization, forests and livelihoods: Theory and narrative', *Global Environmental Change,* vol 17, pp338–348

Taylor, P. L. (2007) 'Conservation, community, and culture? New organizational challenges of community forest concessions in the Maya Biosphere Reserve of Guatemala', paper delivered to the 2007 Congress of the Latin American Studies Association, 5–8 September, Montreal

Taylor, P. L., Cronkleton, P., Barry, D., Stone-Jovicich, S., Schmink, M. (2008) *If You Saw it with My Eyes: Collaborative Research and Assistance with Central American Forest Steward Communities,* CIFOR Forests and Governance Programme Series No 14, Bogor, Indonesia

Tehan, M., Palmer, L., Langton, M. and Mazel, O. (2006) 'Sharing land and resources: Modern agreements and treaties with indigenous people in settler states', in M. Langton, O. Mazel, K. Shain, L. Palmer and M. Tehan (eds) *Settling With Indigenous People: Modern Treaty and Agreement-making,* The Federation Press, Sydney

Tiffen, M., Mortimore, M. and Gichuki, F. (1994) *More People, Less Erosion: Environmental Recovery in Kenya,* John Wiley, London

Tropico Verde (2005) *El proyecto turístico Cuenca del Mirador y las concesiones forestales en la zona de uso múltiple de la Reserva de la Biosfera Maya* [The Mirador Basin tourism project and the forest concessions in the Maya Biosphere Reserve's multiple use zone], Tropico Verde, Flores, Guatemala

Turnbull, C. (1974) *The Mountain People,* Picador, London

UDRSS/VALEURS (2002) 'The economic value of wild resources in Senegal: A preliminary valuation of non-timber forest products, game and freshwater fisheries'. Synthesis report, UDRSS/VALEURS (Utilisation durable des ressources sauvages au Sénégal/valorisation des espèces prior une utilisation durables des resources sauvages au Sénégal)

United Nations (2006) *The Millenium Development Goals Report 2006,* United Nations Department of Economics and Social Affairs (DESA), United Nations, New York

United Nations General Assembly (2005) 'In larger freedom: Towards development, security and human rights for all', report of the Secretary General to the United Nations General Assembly, New York

Uphoff, N. (1986) *Local Institutional Development: An Analytical Sourcebook with Cases,* Kumarian Press, West Hartford, CT

Uphoff, N. (1992) *Local Institutions and Participation for Sustainable Development,* Gatekeeper Series No 31, International Institute for Environment and Development, London

Vayda, A. P. (1983) 'Progressive contextualization: Methods for research in human ecology', *Human Ecology,* vol 11, no 3, pp265–282

Vice President's Office (1997) *National Environmental Policy,* Government Printers, Dar-es-Salaam

Warner, M. (2001) *Complex Problems, Negotiated Solutions: Tools to Reduce Conflict in Community Development,* ITDG Publishing, London

WCD (World Commission on Dams) (2000) *Dams and Development: A New Framework for Decision-Making. An Overview of the Report of the World Commission on Dams,* 16 November, www.dams.org//docs/overview/wcd_overview.pdf, accessed 11 June 2008

WCED (World Commission on Environment and Development) (1987) *Our Common Future,* Oxford University Press, Oxford

Wells, M. P., McShane, T. O., Dublin, H. T., O'Connor, S. and Redford, K. H. (2004) 'The future of integrated conservation and development projects', in T. O. McShane and M. P. Wells (eds) *Getting Biodiversity Projects to Work: Towards More Effective Conservation and Development,* Columbia University Press, New York

Western, D. and Giochio, H. (1993) 'Segregation effects and impoverishment of savanna parks: The case for ecosystem viability analysis', *African Journal of Ecology,* vol 31, pp269–281

Western, D. and Wright, R. W. (1994) 'The background to community-based conservation', in D. Western, R. Wright and S. Strum (eds) *Natural Connections: Perspectives in Community-Based Conservation,* Island Press, Washington DC

Wildlife Conservation Society, International Resources Group, Proyecto FIPA/Guatemala and Consejo Nacional de Areas Protegidas (2003) 'Monitoreo de incendios forestales y estimación de superficies quemadas, Reserva de Biosfera Maya, 2003' [Monitoring of forest fires and estimation of burnt area, Maya Biosphere Reserve, 2003], Wildlife Conservation Society, International Resources Group, Proyecto FIPA/Guatemala, and Consejo Nacional de Areas Protegidas, Petén, Guatemala

Wildlife Conservation Society, Proyecto FIPA/Guatemala International Resources Group and Consejo Nacional de Areas Protegidas (2004) 'Estimación de la deforestación en la Reserva de Biosfera Maya, periodo 2003–2004' [Estimation of deforestation in the Maya Biosphere Reserve, 2003–2004], Wildlife Conservation Society, Proyecto FIPA/Guatemala International Resources Group, and Consejo Nacional de Areas Protegidas, Petén, Guatemala

Wilshusen, P. R., Brechin, S. R., Fortwangler, C. L, and West, P. C. (2003) 'Contested nature: Conservation and development at the turn of the twenty-first century', in S. R. Brechin, P. R. Wilshusen, C. L. Fortwangler and P. C. West (eds) *Contested Nature: Promoting International Biodiversity Conservation with Social Justice in the Twenty-first Century,* State University of New York Press, Albany

Wollenberg, E., Anderson, J. and Edmunds, D. (2001a) 'Pluralism and the less powerful: Accommodating multiple interests in local forest management', *International Journal of Agriculture, Resources, Governance and Ecology (IJARGE),* vol 1, no 3/4, pp199–222

Wollenberg, E., Edmunds, D. and Anderson, J. (2001b) 'Editorial', *International Journal of Agriculture, Resources, Governance and Ecology (IJARGE),* vol 1, no 3/4, pp193–198

World Bank (2001) *World Development Report 2000/2001: Attacking Poverty,* Oxford University Press, New York

World Bank (2004) *Partnerships in Development: Progress in the Fight Against Poverty,* The World Bank, Washington DC

WRI (World Resources Institute) (2005) *The Wealth of the Poor: Managing Ecosystems to Fight Poverty,* World Resources Institute in collaboration with United Nations Development Programme, United Nations Environment Programme and World Bank, World Resources Institute, Washington DC

Wunder, S. (2001) 'Poverty alleviation and tropical forests: What scope for synergies?', *World Development,* vol 29, no 11, pp1817–1833

Wunder, S. (2005) *Payments for Environmental Services: Some Nuts and Bolts,* CIFOR Occasional Paper 42, Center for International Forestry Research, Bogor

WWF (World Wide Fund for Nature) (1965) *The Launching of a New Ark: First Report of the President and Trustees of the World Wildlife Fund 1961–1964,* Collins, London and Glasgow

WWF (1996) *WWF Statement of Principles: Indigenous Peoples and Conservation,* WWF, Gland, Switzerland

Index